stressed out!

out!

FOR PARENTS

stressed out!

FOR PARENTS

HOW TO BE CALM, CONFIDENT, AND FOCUSED

Dr. Ben Bernstein

with Michelle Packard, author of *Family Ever After*

Published by Familius LLC, www.familius.com

Familius books are available at special discounts for bulk purchases for sales promotions, family or corporate use. Special editions, including personalized covers, excerpts of existing books, or books with corporate logos, can be created in large quantities for special needs. For more information, contact Premium Sales at 559-876-2170 or email specialmarkets@familius.com

Library of Congress Catalog-in-Publication Data

2014948916

Paperback ISBN 978-1-939629-31-9
Hardcover ISBN 978-1-942672-53-1
Ebook ISBN 978-1-939629-87-6

Printed in the United States of America

Edited by Michelle Packard and Michele Robbins
Cover Design by David Miles
Book design by Maggie Wickes

10 9 8 7 6 5 4 3 2

First Edition

Contents

For all parents who want to grow with their children.

"If I am not for myself, who will be for me?
If I am only for myself, what am I?
If not now, when?"

—Rabbi Hillel
1st century CE

With Our Thanks

As a psychologist and performance coach, I am deeply grateful to all the parents and children I have worked with over many years who have shared with me their stories, struggles, and triumphs. It has been a privilege to grow with them.

Special thanks to my own family, friends, and colleagues who face the many challenges of parenting on a daily basis: Didi Conn, David Shire, Andrew Bernstein, Mariel Mulet, Richard and Jaimie Bernstein, Joe Ruffatto, Pat Singer, Suzin Green, and David Martin. To my own teachers: Wendla Kernig, David E. Hunt, Viola Spolin, and Catherine Shainberg, I offer my thanks for their encouragement, wisdom and support, as well as to Dr. Tom Phelan, mentor and author.

One of the great pleasures of writing this book has been the opportunity to work with Michelle Packard. Her dedication as a parent, her determination to learn and to grow, and her compassion and skill as a writer suffuse every page of this book. She was the best collaborator I could wish for.

My heartfelt thanks to her. I am forever thankful to my wife, Suk Wah, for her trust and support. Her love inspires me to continue to grow every day.

As co-authors, Michelle and I express our greatest appreciation for the time and effort put forth by the entire Familius team. Heartfelt thanks to Christopher Robins for introducing Michelle to me, and gratitude to his wife, Michele Robbins, for her vision and support of happy families. We so appreciate the time and efforts of David Miles for an inspired cover and to Maggie Wickes for her hours of undoubtedly tedious editing.

And now a note from Michelle . . .

As a mother I have realized that it's rare in life to have anything great come about without the help and support of others. This book is no exception. So much gratitude goes to Ben Bernstein for trusting me with his work of a lifetime. He has truly been a great mentor. Special thanks to my parents Lynne and Byron Hutchings, my siblings and their spouses, James and Liz Hutchings, Heather (who proofed the book cover to cover) and Joe Petersen, Justin and Jodi Hutchings, and Marquie and Patrick Walton, for sharing their stories with me and being great examples of parenthood. Gratitude to Destry Alvarado, Rachelle Christensen and the many other authors, friends, and family who pitched in with a lending ear, personal experiences, and their total honesty.

Most importantly I send my love and appreciation to my children EllaAnne, Daniel, Julia, and Jackson, and to my husband Bryce for being patient with me, allowing me to try out the model with them, and loving me even when I'm not perfect. I can't imagine life without you!

Why Read this Book?

Over forty years ago, I started working as a teacher, psychologist and a coach with children and their parents. The majority of these parents considered being a mom or dad the most important job they'd ever have. Yet early on I recognized that they received little, if any, training in parenting. This is like seating someone behind the wheel of a car and expecting them to drive when they've never even been in a car before! And not just drive, but negotiate a road with unexpected twists and turns, enormous potholes, sudden raging thunderstorms, and goodness-knows-what-else, and, after all that, arrive at their destination intact and unfazed.

As a parent, often the only model you have for parenting are your own parents. My parents—may they rest in peace—were not the best role models. When they married, at a very young age, they were not prepared or trained to take on the responsibilities of parenting. Moreover, their parents also had all kinds of issues, which, in many ways, they passed on to their children.

Before we go any further, I want to state clearly that this is not a book about digging up the past, fault-finding, or placing blame. In fact, we're not going to focus on the past at all except to remember that your model for parenting—for better or worse, and usually both—were your own parents. Since parenting is arguably one of the most demanding jobs ever, you need a more complete toolkit to be best parent you can be. Over the last forty-plus years, through my research, clinical, and personal experience, I've learned what it takes to have a more fulfilling life, and I have coached numerous others along that path. I'm here to help you. Consider me your drivers-ed teacher in parenting.

When parents seek my services as a coach or when I speak publicly, people always ask me, "Do you have kids?" I answer, "It wasn't in our cards." That means that my wife and I, together for over twenty years in a growing and very fulfilling marriage, were not blessed with children. For a variety of reasons, we couldn't avail ourselves of current technologies for conceiving and our circumstances didn't allow for adoption.

When my publisher, Christopher Robbins, approached me about writing this book, I said that I'd like to work on it with someone who is a parent. Even with almost half a century behind me of working with children and their parents, I know having a child or children of your own is very different and personal. I wanted a parent's perspective in this book.

Christopher introduced me to Michelle Packard, who authored *Family Ever After: Simple Ways To Achieve Extraordinary Happiness With Your Ordinary Family*. It's a wonderful book, deeply felt and well written. Michelle is the mother to four young children. I'm delighted and honored that she agreed to co-author this book with me. Since the book you're holding is based on a training model that I've developed through years of research and clinical practice, we have written it in my voice. I'm known as "Dr. B, the Stress Doctor." I'm honored and humbled to offer to you what

I've learned over a lifetime of experience working with people who want to do a better job at parenting.

That said, we thought that this would be a good time for Michelle to introduce herself to you and tell you how she got involved in this project.

HERE'S MICHELLE:

I love families! Really love them. I believe they are the foundation of our lives, and that parents are the foundation of the family. As parents, how we function, manage stress, and connect with our children is, in part, an indication of our happiness. If we are happy in our role as parents, like a pebble tossed in water, that fulfillment will spread to our children, partner, work, friends, involvement in community, and every other aspect of our life. If we are unhappy, the ripple will be a negative one. Finding fulfillment in who we are and what we do in life affects the entire family.

When I was given Dr. B's books, *A Teen's Guide to Success* and *Test Success!*, I embraced them. The more I read the more I wanted, and the more I could see myself and my family in his model of success. I loved his stories and analogies and felt like they were easily compatible and applicable with the stresses that all parents face. So when Dr. B asked me to help him apply his model to parenting, I was in.

I supposed if I was going to write about this, I had better try out the principles and practices. So I did. One Saturday evening after a fun-filled day at the lake I was barraged with stressful parenting situations. My husband had left our play-day early to finish up some things at work, so I was on my own with our four kids. After arriving home and cleaning out the car, my number one priority was to clear out the pile of dirty dishes stacked up in the kitchen sink. My plan was to divide and conquer with the children's help. There was just one problem; the kids didn't want to help. They were too tired.

Then the meltdowns began. My older son was upset because school started Monday, and he needed a haircut. My two-year-old somehow ripped his fingernail off and was spilling tears. My five-year-old fell outside and scraped her knee, and, of course, there were more tears, very tired tears. To top it off my oldest daughter wasn't feeling well and was sure she was going to throw up. Bedtime was fast approaching, and the kids still needed baths and dinner. I stayed calm for a while, but as the kids became more upset, so did I.

I was adamant about finishing the dishes, because I was tired, too, and didn't want to wake up the next morning to a mess. Even though the kids needed me, I just wanted them to disappear for fifteen minutes before they sucked all the life out of me. Suddenly, I realized this was a perfect moment to see if Dr. B's model really worked. Without giving too much away here, I focused on his three keys to success under stress: being calm, remaining confident, and staying focused.

The first thing I noticed was that I was very focused but on the wrong thing. It was my children who needed my focus, not the dishes. I was also feeling overwhelmed, lacking the confidence to deal with everything. I wished my husband would sail through the door and save me, but, since that wasn't likely, I had to try something different. I had to muster up my own confidence. Following Dr. B's model, I thought to myself, *The kids have been like this before, and you handled it well. You know what to do. Start with the most urgent need and work your way through it. You can do this.*

Something incredible happened. I really knew I could do it, and so I began. I scooped up my two-year-old, bandaged his wounded fingernail and grabbed extra Band-Aids for my five-year-old. I cleaned her up, then spent some time holding, calming, and loving both of them. I had my oldest lie down until I could help her and told my son I would cut his hair when the youngest two were in bed. By using Dr. B's tools, I saw an immediate lowering of my stress level and an improvement in my behavior.

I was calm and gentle with the kids, and they began to calm down. They could see I was focused on them. They were confident in me because I took control of the situation. Everything got done, everyone was happier, and I would say we had a successful evening.

Since receiving my degree in home and family science, I have had the opportunity to work with numerous young children, adolescents, and adults as a counselor. I have written a book on family life, and have oodles of hands-on experience with parenting. There were times as a parent when I had used some of the tools and principles Dr. B teaches, without really understanding what I was doing. I wish that through all these experiences I had had Dr. B's model of success. It is one of the most unique and helpful systems I have ever found for parenting and for life in general. It has empowered me to be a better parent. If Dr. B's model can change and improve this one instance in my life so quickly, I know it can change the lives of parents all over the world.

It is our hope to share this model with you, to help you be truly happy and fulfilled as a parent and a human being. Dr. B and I have spent hours relating experiences, interviewing parents, and practicing the principles of the model as it pertains to parenting. Dr. B coached others and me on how to improve our use of the model, so that we could share it with you.

We have changed names of parents and children in order to protect privacy. Many of my thoughts and experiences are quietly embedded in Dr. B's wisdom and model of success. Together we have been able to create something that really works. Use it, learn from it, and see the changes in yourself and your family, as I have seen in mine.

AND NOW, BACK TO DR. B.:

I am most grateful to Michelle for giving herself to this project and using the model with her own family. It helps ground everything we've written about in this book. That means what you're about to read is not a collection of "Good Ideas." As a parent you don't need more ideas. You need practical coaching to aid you in dealing with the daily stresses of being a parent. That's what this book is designed to do.

This book offers you useful tools. By following the coaching, you'll become more aware and observant—more conscious—of where things are going and where you'd like them to go. You'll be that much more prepared to be behind the wheel with any kind of road conditions, in any kind of weather, with whomever is in the car.

As we begin this journey together, we recommend that you take a moment to start a journal. Any kind—computer, notebook, iPad—whatever your preference, and keep it with you as you read. Your journal will be a safe, private place for you to go and reflect on what we'll be looking at together. We have also added some Question and Answer dialogue between myself and Michelle at the end of chapters. You will recognize this dialogue by the symbol Q & A.

Are you ready? Let's go.

CHAPTER 1

Becoming the Parent You Want to Be

YOU HAVE A LOT GOING ON

Your toddler is crying because his brother just grabbed his favorite toy, the school is calling because your delinquent teenager cut classes again, and your office is texting to let you know you have to work late tomorrow, which means you'll miss your daughter's soccer game. Your kids spend more time with Facebook than they do with you. In fact, you know your son is watching a movie at his girlfriend's house only because he posted it on his page. You're wife thinks you're too hard on the kids, and you're tired of the kids taking all of her extra time. And everyone wants money. Money! You're never going to have enough money to pay for the broken bones, windows, and glasses frames. College? Well you're definitely not going to be able to afford that. You're a dinosaur when it comes to technology. You're always tired. You feel guilty when you're at work because you aren't with your kids, and you feel guilty when you are with your kids because you are not doing more at work. But what does that really matter? Your kids would rather hang out with their friends. You rarely have time with your spouse, and you can't seem to get to all those "extra" tasks. You're worried your kids are being bullied at school; you're worried they don't have any friends; you're worried you are going to mess them up before they ever have a chance at life.

How can you manage it all? How can you possibly succeed at parenting?

CALM, CONFIDENT, AND FOCUSED

In this book I'm going to give you the three keys to being a successful parent. You already know them from the book's subtitle, so my cards are on the table. When you learn—really learn—to be calm, confident, and focused in your parenting, you'll be amazed at how much you can handle, and not just handle but do really well.

Being calm, remaining confident, and staying focused are the three keys to success in any endeavor of life.

How do I know this? I've been a psychologist and teacher for over forty years, and my area of specialization is success and how people become successful. To figure this out, I've studied, observed, and coached people in many fields—sports, business, teaching, healthcare, the performing arts, and parenting to name a few. Over and over again I've seen that every successful person has built a strong foundation that doesn't depend on whether they have lived a less-than-privileged life or if they were given a better lot at birth. It doesn't matter if people have "talent" or not, if they're patient or compassionate, or good with kids or indifferent. It doesn't even matter if they have failed many times. What matters is this: that they have learned how to be calm, confident, and focused.

Here's an example of what I'm talking about from a parenting perspective:

As the telephone rings, Ethan, age eight, runs into the house with a look of sheer panic on his face. His friends, all looking worried, trail closely behind him. Ethan's mother, Amy, knows the incoming phone call is from the neighbors, and it's going to be bad news. As she picks up the phone her fears are confirmed. Filled with embarrassment, her heart rate jumps, her fists clench, and her brow furrows. She slams the phone down on the counter and starts berating Ethan for shattering the neighbors' new sliding glass patio door. She starts yelling, "You never stop and think! You are so irresponsible! How could you throw a rock through their glass door? I give you so much, and this is the thanks I get?" Ethan starts crying, and Amy sends him to his room. Suddenly, she is brought back to reality by the fearful and silent wide eyes of the neighbors' children who have been watching this whole scenario. Embarrassed, her heart drops, her shoulders fall, and her brow settles as she begins to feel the weight, guilt, and stress of failure.

In contrast, a few houses down, Jenny's son Derek quietly comes in the house trailed by his friends. "Derek broke the neighbor's windshield. He was throwing rocks over the house, and he shattered it!"

Jenny observes how upset Derek is and lets him speak immediately. He nervously admits that he shattered the neighbor's windshield because he and his friends were seeing if they could throw a rock all the way over the house, not aware that the car was on the other side. Jenny's first response is to pause. She takes a deep breath. She thinks, *How should I react to this? What do I want Derek to learn? How do I teach him and show him that I still love him?* While she expresses appreciation for his honesty, she begins to feel stressed. She knows she will inevitably have to come up with the money to pay for the windshield. She can tell her stress is increasing because she's

3

not breathing regularly. So she calms herself with a deep breath and the inner reaffirmation: *It will work out. It always does. Derek didn't mean to break the window, and he is a good kid. It was very brave of him to tell the truth.* Jenny expresses these feelings to her son calmly. She discusses the broken windshield with him and asks him what he needs to do to make recompense for his actions. Jenny and Derek then go to the neighbors, and he apologizes. Derek sticks to the plan he created with his mom and gives the neighbors all the money he has—one dollar. Mom cuts a check for the broken windshield. Derek has promised to pay the rest back to her. Jenny helps Derek clean up the glass. She then focuses on teaching Derek to make smarter choices that involve thinking about the possible consequences of his actions. Though everything is far from perfect, Jenny feels good about the outcome, and Derek has learned about being responsible for his actions.

Simply put, Jenny is calm, confident, and focused in this situation. Amy is not. Because of this, Ethan is afraid to go to his mom when things turn for the worse (which, for a parent feels like failure), while Derek feels safe in going to his mother even when he knows he will be in trouble (success for the parent). Both parents are in similar circumstances, but their parenting experience is very different. Jenny has practiced using the tools, so that they have become second nature to her.

You, too, can learn to use these tools in your parenting and be successful.

WHAT IS "SUCCESS"?

Jenae, mother of four, admitted how much she loved bedtime, simply because she could check out, even if only for a moment. She longed for the crying to stop, the whining to cease, the pleas for help to vaporize, and the constant requests for time and money to end.

Like Jenae, nearly everyone moans at some time or another about how hard it is to raise children. Toddlers moan, teenagers moan, parents moan.

Erma Bombeck, a famous American housewife and columnist, said of parenting, "I take a very practical view of raising children. I put a sign in each of their rooms: checkout time is eighteen years. Parents can become so consumed by the stresses of parenting for those eighteen years that often they check out before their children."

While it might not seem feasible now, I can assure you that as you learn and use the tools I'm offering you in this book, these parenting years will become much more an adventure than an endurance contest for you and for everyone in your life. If you find yourself needing to check out for a moment, don't postpone too long before you check back in. You can't be successful at something you're not doing.

As you experience success now—and not have to wait until you're children are grown—your world will open up. Rather than feel like life is just too much and you want to check out—and who doesn't sometimes?— you will take on the challenges of being and becoming the best parent you can be, knowing that you are successfully teaching, loving, and preparing your children for a successful life as well as finding fulfillment along the way.

Let's pause for a moment and consider what I mean by "success." Conventionally, the word conjures up a pile of money, a fabulous car, a big house, the ability to travel, and having lots of things. As a parent it could also include having children who excel academically, are involved in a number of extracurricular activities, and are one hundred percent competent and trustworthy. While there's nothing wrong with any of this, what I mean by "success" is actually much deeper and more lasting. To me, success means being happy and feeling fulfilled. If you're thinking, *Well, I'd be happy with a Ferrari!* I won't argue with you. I'd be happy with one too. But lasting happiness never came from owning a great car, having a lot of money, having fabulous good looks, or even from raising perfect children. It comes from owning yourself. It comes from being fully you.

As you read that last sentence you may have been thinking, *Ugh. He doesn't get it. I can't be a mom or dad and fully me at the same time. I don't have time to be at every soccer game, my house is never clean, my kids always yell at me, and I'm not the good looking gal I used to be. I really don't like my life or myself. I don't make delicious pies like Mary. My kids are not in the élite choir like Steve's. My clothes are never top of the line like Susie's, and we never seem to be able to make ends meet.* All that may be true. But saying "I'm not this" or "I'm not that" just gets you tied up in "nots" (excuse the pun). You aren't giving any positive attention to who you are. The truth is you will never be like Mary, Steve, or Susie, and your kids will never be like their kids. Why? Because you're you. You might as well accept and like who you are and what you have. Stop comparing, stop whining, and get with your own parenting program. Unless you do—and until you do—you're not going to be happy.

I asked Michelle, my co-author, to tell me about how she discovered this. Here's what she said:

> After the birth of my fourth child I was one hundred percent wiped. Recovery did not come easily and eventually turned into a life of just getting by, and just getting by meant letting things go. I would go to the store in my fat jeans, followed by my sorry looking gang. One child would be missing his socks, the other hadn't brushed her teeth for what seemed like a week, I forgot to brush the little one's hair, and it went on and on. The kids were very happy in their sorry state. I was the only one who cared. Well, me and all the grandmas who gave me dirty looks.
>
> As I walked through the store trying to get in and out with the least notice of my gang and me, I would watch these skinny women in their cute trendy clothes. Their well-groomed children—that all the grandmas smiled at—in tow. Oh how I wanted that. It was in these pathetic moments I longed for my old body, my old energy, and my old but younger me. The cute one, who remembered things, who had it together, and who wasn't so tired.

After so many visits to the grocery store these comparisons wore on me. I was tired of them, and I was tired of not being successful in my venture of parenthood. So I just told myself, *That's it. You are not those women, and no matter how long you go to bed hungry, you will not have their metabolism. Their children are not your children, so stop comparing. Your children are happy, well fed, usually well groomed, and their grandmas love them perfectly. If you don't like how things are going, change them but not by what you envision skinny women standards are, but by your own standards.*

I'm not so sure a whole lot of things changed right away, but my attitude did. As I persisted in working towards the life I wanted, my focus changed and so did my direction as a parent and a person. My children still sometimes show up at the store without socks or perfect hair. I'm still six sizes larger than the skinny people, but I am happy being me. I am happy as a parent, and I am happy with my life. I consider that a success.

You will save yourself a lot of time, energy, and heartache if you learn how to be happy with who you are and the family you have. Now. No matter how bad you feel at times—and parenting can plunge you into many a pit of bad feelings—you are not that mess of unhappiness. If that sounds like I'm saying, "Just get through these parenting years," I'm not. I'm saying that the happy, child-free adult you once were in the past and the happy grandparent you may be one day in the future are connected by the parent you are right now. You can be a miserable parent, or you can be a happy, successful one. I'll say it again: you can be happy and you can be successful right now. You don't have to suffer through your child-rearing years. Now is the only time you have, and now is the time to begin living, consciously, by choice, into the fullness of who you are and the parent you want to be.

Happiness—what I'm calling "success"—will be yours as you learn to be more calm, confident, and focused. I know this because I've coached many people like you to live this way, and their lives have blossomed.

HOW TO HANDLE STRESS

In this book I'm going to take you through a process. We'll look at how you handle parenting challenges and, particularly, how you handle stress. For instance, if you have a disagreement with your child do you become anxious and tense and start yelling, or do you know how to stay calm and work it through? If you are facing an important challenge—your toddler is injured, your teenager is demanding more money, or you don't have enough time to spend with your family—do you doubt whether you can handle it, or do you have the confidence that you can perform well? When you have tough decisions to make about what activities to let your children participate in or whom to let your daughter date, do you let the situation take charge of you, or are you focused and intentional about positive solutions?

You may have noticed that the title of this book isn't *Dr. B's Bag of Magic Tricks for Parents*. There's no kit with a top hat and a wand that you wave over your head and then—presto! You can now sail through your parenting years without doing anything differently. My job as a coach is to show you what to do. Your job is to do it. For many, that's not an easy thing. They would prefer if their children just stopped creating problems for them to solve. I admit that would be nice, but we all know it won't happen.

I have discovered that there are two groups of people: those who are ready to work for change and those who want a quick fix. The latter often come into my office cramped with anxiety or gloomy with depression. After the first session, they are filled with hope and enthusiasm. They come to the second session all pumped up saying, "This is great. I get it." But several weeks later they call or email, moaning in a most painful way, "Oh, Dr. B, I'm still so stressed out! I'm messing up. Everything's going down the tubes! I haven't done any of the exercises you gave me. Do you have any more tips?"

Yes, I do have more "tips," but what good will new tips do if you won't put to use the original ones. If you want positive results, you have to follow the coaching. Ultimately, you have to become your own coach. There's no way around it. And if you do, the rewards are great. I have watched parents turn around their relationships with their children. I've seen these same parents find fulfillment in who they are. I've seen these parents' children follow in their parents' footsteps of success. The bottom line is this: parents who practice being calm, confident, and focused become their personal best by working through and overcoming challenges.

BE PRESENT

In facing challenges, we learn life's most important lesson: be present. You know that phrase they use at raffles, "You have to be present to win."? The same is true of parenting. Only by being present can we develop the awareness that we're veering off track, and then get back on track. How many times as a parent have you had to admit that you screwed up because you didn't show up?

Jarin was consumed in power washing the deck. He was in a hurry, as he had a long list of things to accomplish on his day off. His thoughts would bounce from how awful the deck looked to how fantastic the deck will look when he was done, to what he would need to buy for his next project. Sporadically he would think, *I should check on Haden,* but he pushed away the thoughts. When his three-year-old son dumped the can of sealant—meant for the deck—all over the grass and himself, Jarin was concerned and upset. Had Jarin become aware of what the inner voice of his spirit was telling him, to check on Haden, and acted on his awareness, he would have had an entirely different experience. Jarin screwed up because he didn't show up.

There is a real correlation between awareness and excellence, but awareness doesn't happen accidentally. Usually, our minds are wandering far from home, leap-frogging from the past into the future, oblivious to what's in front of us. To cultivate awareness and achieve your highest potential, you have to train yourself to bring your awareness to bear on the present moment and to practice being calm, confident, and focused right now. When you learn how to master yourself, you will feel empowered to take these skills into any part of your life. You will have taught yourself to be strong, responsible, and embodied when confronted with a difficult child or a challenging undertaking—like parenting. You can use that knowledge anywhere you go. And in doing so, you become a positive, resourceful role model for your own children.

A good part of this process is you becoming more aware of yourself. As long as you are willing to do the work to become a success, you will find success.

THE PURPOSE OF PARENTING

Before we move on, I want to ask you a question: have you ever wondered what the purpose of your life is as a parent? Here's what I say: The purpose of your life as a parent is to cultivate your children to become good people and eventually be good parents themselves. It is to walk side-by-side with your children and help them through their challenges and make a positive contribution to your family and the world. Parenting is about learning what real love is and learning how to share it. It is about giving your whole self to something greater than yourself and in the process becoming and being your highest self. It is about living the life you teach about and joyfully sharing that life with your children.

When you want a flower to grow in your garden, you go to the nursery and buy a packet of seeds. You can see exactly what you're going to end up with because there is a beautiful color picture of the fully-grown flower on the front of the packet. But when you open it, what do you find? Tiny black lumps that look like mouse droppings. Does that discourage you? No, because you know what these seeds are meant to become. You set up the environment for the seeds to grow. You prepare the soil. You plant the seed and then make sure you give it the right amount of sunlight and water.

When that tiny seedling finally sprouts, it is delicate, and you protect it and care for it until it grows into the flower it is meant to be. It takes its place in the garden and is part of a thriving landscape.

I believe that somewhere inside you there is a seed packet with your picture on it, a picture of the fully realized you as a successful parent. It's not easy to grow this flower. There are challenges all along the way. But when you face them, you learn from them, and you grow with them. Through this process, you grow into the flower in full bloom. Flowers cannot become fully realized unless they push their way up through the soil and share the sun and space with other plants. Our conditions aren't much different. We have to find our way in the world and in our families, and all along we face challenges—a rebellious child, presentations or deadlines at work, familial breakdowns, physical illness, a disabled child, financial reversals, unfulfilled expectations, and loss. You may even feel like your once beautiful petals have wilted or fallen, but the wonderful part about a flower is that it can rejuvenate itself.

Though we cannot choose most of the challenges we face in life—and that's particularly true as parents—we can choose how we're going to face them. Are we going to have a bad experience, crumble under the pressure, check out early, or avoid challenges altogether? Or are we going to find the strength and inner resources to rise to the challenges and fully actualize our potential as parents? That's the term psychologists use for becoming the person, and I would add parent, you are meant to be. Facing your child rearing years—and sometimes beyond—in a productive way will give you this opportunity. The challenges in your life require you to call on the inner resources residing deep inside you. By doing that, you come to know yourself and develop your innate capacities. That is what we mean by actualizing your potential, and being challenged presents you with the opportunities to do it.

Fortunately, we don't have to reinvent the wheel here. There are exquisite role models who have preceded us and can show us how to face the ups and downs of life in a meaningful way. These are the parents and grandparents who never give up. The teachers and masters, saints and sages, the divinely inspired women and men who dedicated their lives to finding meaning and purpose through their struggles. Each faced the challenges that life handed them, and they mastered the ability to learn and grow and become fully realized beings. We may not all be sages and saints, but we all face challenges on a regular basis, and some of them are severe and daunting. Do we have the strength to overcome, the fortitude to persevere, the humor to see things in a lighter way? With these capacities, it is possible to do more than just get by. We can do something inspiring with our lives. Great beings create a memorable path through life's tests. Because ultimately, that's what life is—a path with tests at every bend in the road. And every test is there to help us grow and to fully become the parent we are meant to be.

The word "parent" spans a lifetime that is momentous, tumultuous, and varied. The experiences of someone with a newborn just trying to make it through the night are vastly different than that of the parent of three teenagers: one who is learning to drive, one who is seriously dating a girl, and one who is vying for a scholarship to college. As you'll soon see, what I am offering are life skills. I am trusting that you, the reader, will apply the insights and tools given here at whatever point you are in this span of great growth and transformation called parenthood. It is your life, after all, and you are in the driver's seat. You can learn to be a calm, confident, and focused parent.

You are meant to be successful.

CHAPTER 2

Performance and Stress

Across the board, in every field of human endeavor, there is one factor that affects performance positively and negatively, and that is stress. We often assume that success means learning the subject matter. But I've seen scores of people who are very knowledgeable and experienced at what they do—whether it's playing the trumpet or being a swimmer—but when it comes time to perform, they stress out and lose it. Why is this important? Because when you have to deal with a difficult situation—when you have to perform as a parent—the way you feel about yourself and your ability as a parent to stay grounded and present largely determines how successful you will be. Understand that the quality of the experience in any challenge directly affects the results.

The reason for this is simple: stress affects performance. This is well known in many fields, especially in sports. Athletes need a certain amount of stress to charge them up, so they can perform at their best. If the stress crosses a certain line—either too much stress or too little—it starts hurting their ability to do well. This concept is known as the "zone of optimal functioning."

WHAT IS STRESS?

When I begin coaching my clients, the first question I always ask them is, "What do you think causes your stress as a parent?" Here are some of the things they tell me:

(Which statements apply to you?)

- My kids won't do their homework.
- I'm not giving my kids enough quality time.
- The kids are always fighting.
- I'm not giving my paid work enough time.
- The kids like my spouse's parents more than mine.
- My children are always making a mess, which means more work for me.
- I don't have enough intimate time with my spouse (and when we do we're too tired!).
- All my kids want to do is play video games.
- My kids fight me every time I ask them to help out with anything.
- My spouse and I discipline with totally different styles.
- My kids don't have any friends.
- My parents are always giving unwanted and unhelpful advice.
- I say one thing, my kids do another.
- I have very limited time with children because of outside work/ responsibilities.
- My spouse and I argue over who takes care of what—who goes to the baseball game? who talks with the teacher? who makes the kids do their homework?
- When I tell my kids "no," my parents go behind my back.

- My mom has a lot of health problems and needs a lot of my time.
- We are always eating out because there is just no time to prepare food.
- I never have time for myself—someone always needs me.
- I'm so worried about the kids I can't stay focused on work when I'm at work.
- There is so much family drama.

When you hear statements like these, you're probably thinking, Yep, that just about covers all the bases. But what if I told you those weren't the bases? What if I said none of those "reasons" are actually the cause of your stress?

We all seem to think that our stress comes from our children or spouse or our own parents, too little time, exorbitant expectations, unfavorable comparisons with others, and so on. I know it looks as if these conditions are the source of your stress, but they aren't. These are merely part and parcel of living. They include all the conditions of your life. Conditions in and of themselves do not cause stress. If they did, everyone who lived under the same conditions would react exactly the same way and succumb to stress. As you'll see, this is not the case. Many people have the ability to successfully manage the conditions.

I can hear you thinking, but all of those things really do cause a lot of stress in my life. There's no question about it. Life is stressful. As you'll see, I have a different theory about what causes stress. It starts with looking at what you are doing when you face something challenging or difficult.

GET INTO "THE ZONE"

The amount of stress needed to produce optimal performance, the amount considered healthful, is different for each person. Some people have to feel extremely worked up to jump-start themselves to perform well. Others will feel rattled and nervous with that much stress. For each person there is a zone of optimal functioning where the level of stress is just right. They are stimulated just enough to be creative and energized, to solve problems rationally, and to achieve a sense of self-satisfaction in their performance. Their adrenaline is not pumping too hard, nor are they lethargic, so they are able to progress at a good rate.

Becoming calm, confident, and focused is how you as a parent will find and stay in your zone of optimal functioning. By reading the examples and doing the exercises in this book, you can learn how to control stress rather than let it control you. It's unrealistic to think you won't have any stress. But you need to know how to keep your stress at an optimal level so that it charges you up and keeps you at the top of your game rather than letting it wear you out, make you perform sub-optimally, and run you into the ground.

PERFORMING OPTIMALLY

The relationship between stress and performance is one of the most thoroughly researched phenomena in the field of psychology. It was first investigated over a hundred years ago, and it looks like this:

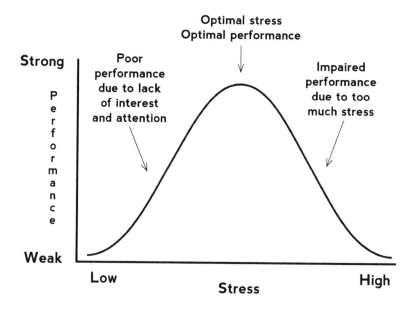

As you can see, when your stress as a parent escalates to the point of discomfort, your effectiveness diminishes. When there's too much stress, you leave "the optimal zone." The result is your problem-solving skills contract and your self-esteem and confidence decline. You have trouble staying focused, so you feel tense, sometimes to the point of feeling sick or exhausted. At this point, your temper is short, fuses blow, and your performance plummets. Here's a scenario:

Your son has to make a mural for his school project. He needs modeling clay, glue, a shoebox, and some popsicle sticks. You figure the project isn't due for two weeks, so why rush to the store to buy it now. You're not under any stress to get this done. So you don't. As the date approaches you forget about it. Your son continues to remind you, but you are sidetracked by so many other more pressing things. Before you know it, it's the night before the project is due, and there are no supplies. Your son is upset, you are tired, and you are both arguing. Accusations are flying. You ask your child, "Why didn't you start on this sooner?" To which he responds, "Why didn't you get the supplies? I reminded you." Suddenly there is too much stress, and you are losing it over a few art supplies. You did not perform well.

This relationship between stress and performance holds true whether you are putting the kids to bed, starting a new job, or having a heated discussion with your spouse or partner. Again, to most people, a performance suggests something that happens on a stage or an athletic field. But if we think of performance as an action, an act of carrying out something, performance involves learning how to be fully present, at whatever you're doing, in the moment, right there when you have to act. It doesn't matter how well you did something last week, or how well you will do tomorrow; the only thing that counts is how you perform now. This state of performing at your best in the present moment is well known to athletes, stage performers, surgeons, and many, many others who must bring their knowledge, training, and experience to bear right now. I want you, as a parent, to refine this skill as well. That way, the outer conditions can change (they always do), but you remain consistently you, performing at your best.

Remember, knowing and performing are not the same thing. When you're upset with your child, knowing you shouldn't yell is not the same as practicing staying grounded and centered (even if you feel angry). Performing refers to what you do with what you know. The primary complaint I hear from parents that I coach is that they know what they should do, but when faced with a challenge they get "stressed out" and can't perform well—they know they shouldn't yell, but when they are stressed they do it anyway. To be successful, you have to deliver what you know. It is essential that you learn how to recognize stress and reduce it, so that the stress is not destructive.

ARE YOU A STRESSED PARENT?

How many of the following scenarios do you identify with?

- Are you angry with your kids when they start crying because you told them they had to put a seat belt on?
- Does your heart beat faster when they turn their backs to you and moan about how they hate school every morning when they have to wake up?
- Do you get a headache when your children beg for money, and then tell you that you don't care about them because you're not handing it over?
- Do you feel hopeless or betrayed when you tell your kids they can't go to their friend's house and your spouse lets them go anyway?
- Do you get angry when your wife lets your daughter wear a mini skirt when you know exactly what *those* boys are thinking?
- Do you grit your teeth when Grandma—your mom! —continues to give junk food to your kids?
- Does your body temperature rise and your face feel hot every time you have to explain to the kids why their uncle is in jail?
- Do you feel defensive and annoyed that you can't take the kids on

vacation without visiting the extended family?

- Are you arguing over who leaves work early to stay home with sick kids?
- Do you feel frazzled and tense after work when you find yourself in high demand with your children?

All of the above situations are things that are happening outside of you. They are real and legitimate, but they are events you cannot control. You can't help it if your toddler puts up a fight to put her seatbelt on or if your son hates getting out of bed every morning. You can't make your spouse agree with you over every item of clothing your children wear. You can, however, control *your* response to such situations, and this is what we are here to work on. Becoming aggressive, tense, or having an increased heart rate are controllable responses.

Being a parent is different than any other job you will ever perform, because once it begins it never ends. You can't clock out at 5 pm every day and take the weekends off. Even when you sleep you are not free from parenthood—someone has a bad dream, someone is sick, or someone is missing his or her curfew. And once the kids are safe at home and asleep they are always running through your mind—*Sarah didn't finish her school project. I don't think that Jenny is a good influence on my son.* and *Why won't Josh talk to me anymore?* Kids are draining and wonderful all at the same time. You also have to learn to work with your partner, and sometimes that's just hard. Then, there are always extended family matters to consider. And finding any kind of work-life balance is a monumental task that can feel impossible. Performing at your peak level is all about reducing your stress from the events that so consistently bombard you as a parent.

HUMAN PERFORMANCE

I work with teenagers, parents, surgeons, actors, athletes, executives, and all kinds of people who face life's tests on a daily basis. I'm often asked,

"How can you coach so many different people?" "How can you help a golfer improve her golf game? Do you play golf?" "How can you help a parent discipline more effectively? Do you know all about parenting?"

Here's what I answer: "I know about human performance and what everyone needs to perform at his or her best." While I don't know as much as the people who come to coach with me—I don't play golf, I never filled a tooth, and I am not a parent—I know what makes performance successful. Of course, the next question is, "And what is that?"

The answer is simple. The common denominator across every field of human endeavor is the person. In your case, it's you as a parent. You may well ask, "What does being a parent have to do with performance?"

The dictionary defines the word "performance" as the action or process of carrying out or accomplishing an action, task, or function, and I think of performance in this broad way. In other words, no matter what you're doing—whether you are clothes shopping with your teenage daughter, trying to protect your toddler from inappropriate media, paying for a child's broken arm, running your kids to soccer practice, or arguing about cell phone use—you are performing. Think of your performance as the act of being and becoming a better parent. Your children are performing as children, and you are performing as a parent. Successful performance means that you are accomplishing your task well.

THE CONSTANT IS YOU

When a parent comes to me for performance coaching, my first thought is: *What does this person need to perform at his or her best?* Of course, parents have to learn specifics—when to feed their baby solids, methods of disciplining, and how to listen effectively—but that is only part of the picture. As you know from your experience as a parent, life is always changing. Your teenager might be doing great at school one day, and the next day her friends gossip about her, and she comes home a basket case. You might think you are good at showing love to your child until he comes to you one morning and tells you he feels like you don't care about him.

> John gave an example, saying, "I have always prided myself in being the kind of parent my kids could talk to. That is until one evening I was stressed about a deadline at work. My daughter wanted to talk about something and I was ornery with her, trying to get her in and out as fast as possible. She was upset and told me, 'I just won't talk to you then!' Not what a dad wants to hear. My great track record felt like it went down the tubes."

There is one thing that doesn't change, one constant at the center of everything you do in life, no matter what the specifics, no matter what the setting. That constant is you, the parent. When I say, "The constant is you," I mean that you are what is certain and continual in every encounter you face as a parent. Certainty refers to something that stays the same in spite of outer conditions. There might be a deadline at work, an emergency visit to the ER with your kid, or a relationship issue with your child or spouse. Whatever the challenge is for you, you are the one who is facing it.

The question you have to ask yourself is this: *What can I learn about myself that will help me perform better in any parenting situation? How can I take control of this process?*

Imagine what it would be like to have the firm faith that you will succeed under any circumstances: when your child is throwing the biggest tantrum of his life on the floor of the grocery store and you're tired, embarrassed, and feel pressure from the dirty looks judging you as a parent; when your teenage daughter gets pregnant and you feel like you've failed and are overwhelmed with your inability to handle the situation; you get overly involved at your son's basketball game to his great embarrassment and that of the team, or in an argument with your children, you suddenly give up because you feel like you have lost the power to convince them of anything. Whatever the challenge, whatever the environment, you can be constant in yourself as a parent so you can perform at your best.

BECOMING AWARE

When a father is upset at his son's laziness and unable to control his temper when his son refuses to do his homework, or a mother is at her wit's end, unable to stay calm when disciplining her child, I give them the tools to change their reactions—to be less stressed. Providing tools is a vital part of my job as a coach. Think of the book you are holding as a toolbox. In the following pages we will discuss the nine essential tools you need to reduce your stress as a parent, improve your parenting skills, and, in turn, your life. But a shiny new toolbox with powerful tools is not enough. You have to know when to use them. There's a right moment to use each tool in this book, and it is important to your success to develop your awareness of that moment. When your awareness is keen, the tools become indispensable.

When Rosa was trying to get her nine-year-old son Justin to sit down and do his homework, he refused. After some persistence she finally got him to comply but the moment she turned her back he would run outside to play, go to the bathroom, or sneak off to play a video game. She was increasingly annoyed, and the situation was becoming too much for her to handle. She felt stressed and began to mumble, "Is this really worth all the frustration? I'll never get this parenting thing right. My son has no respect for me!" Rosa had recently learned the tools of being confident but had not remembered to use them. Had she refined her awareness skill and recognized that her confidence was slipping, she could have used the correct tools to recover it.

Awareness is another word for paying attention. As parents you are constantly driving down a road with signs that shout, "DANGER AHEAD!" But you don't always see them. The signs become bigger, and maybe you see them but don't take them seriously. What happens? You crash. When you read the signs (that's your awareness) and manipulate the car accordingly (those are the tools) you can look forward to a safer, more pleasant journey.

If you have the greatest tool but lack the awareness of when to use it, the tool is useless. Imagine a baseball player who is up to bat. He has the tools he needs (a bat) to hit the ball, but if he doesn't know when and how to swing, the tools are useless. He will strike out every time. Likewise if you are aware that you need tools but don't have any, you can't change anything. This would be like going up to bat without any tools, in this case the bat.

QUESTION & ANSWER

Michelle: Dr. B, we have discussed that parents often feel stressed because we know what to do in a parenting situation, but fail to act. However, I often feel stressed with my children because I simply don't know what to do. I'm faced with unfamiliar situations almost every day. What do I do when I don't know what to do? How do I manage my stress?

Dr B: This is a great question and affects every parent at some time. But it suggests you should know everything, and how to handle every situation, which, of course, you can't. Whatever the outer circumstances, no matter how small or serious, common or unusual, there's one thing you *can* know, which is yourself, and how to respond to stress producing situations in a calm, confident, and focused way. That's what this book will give you: the tools for reducing your stress in *any* situation, however unfamiliar it is, so that you can perform optimally. Notice that I said "reduce" your stress, not "manage" it (as you asked in your question). Managing stress sounds like it's a force outside of you with a life of its own. As you'll see, it's not. When you learn to reduce your feeling of being stressed—when you learn to be calm, confident, and focused in stress producing situations—you'll be able to access the resources and support you need for any situation, however unfamiliar.

CHAPTER 3

You're Stressed because You're Disconnecting

Trina is upset with her toddler—he keeps climbing on things, and she's worried he's going to fall and get hurt.

Abe doesn't know how to handle his demanding teenager and storms away from their conversation mumbling under his breath.

Karen feels her spouse is being inconsiderate—he's never around to help with the kids—and she shuts down and gives him the silent treatment.

All of these scenarios have something in common. They began as conditions that existed outside of the skin, and each has an element that cannot be controlled by the parent. Trina can't stop her toddler's desire to climb. Abe can't control his son's demands, and Karen can't make her husband help with the kids. Though these can be frustrating conditions, they did not become so until these people let the situation get under their skin. Without being aware of what they were doing, they transformed their external factors to internal problems.

In any parenting situation, you will have a reaction to outside events, and it will either be pleasant, unpleasant, or neutral. That's the range. When your reaction is unpleasant, that's what we call stress because it causes you to reject what's happening. The string of thoughts goes something like this: *I don't like what's going on. Something is wrong. I want this situation to change. I want it to go away.* The first clue that an outside event is causing a stress reaction is that all of a sudden, you cannot relax, and you want things to be different. You can't accept this moment just as it is. Whenever something has to change or you won't be happy, that is the experience of stress.

Not everyone has an unpleasant reaction to the same events. Imagine two parents at the same baseball game cheering on their kids. When Eric's son, Bradley, strikes out at bat, Eric's entire body becomes tense. He yells at Bradley and becomes discouraged, replaying the strikeout over and over in his mind. Jeff, on the other hand, cheers on his son, Todd, even when Todd misses pitch after pitch. Jeff pulls Todd aside for a moment, talks him through his swing, and tells him to keep his head in the game—in a calm, confident, and focused way.

Many parents at the ball game will identify with Eric. They exhibit physical symptoms (headache, clenched fists, stiff neck), they are full of doubt in their child's capabilities, and they are so stuck on the strikeout they can't enjoy the rest of the game. The result is they are unhappy and possibly embarrassed. They fail to support their child successfully, and can't enjoy the game. They have flopped at their attempt at good parenting despite their effort to be there and support their budding baseball player.

Maybe they manage to remain respectable in spite of the strains upon them. But there's hidden damage. They may look well, but they suffer emotionally.

They feel the pressure their child is under, and it causes a great deal of anguish and anxiety, yet they still manage to be fairly successful at supporting their child game after game. They don't do anything about their discomfort because they don't think that it can change. When I ask about the possibility of improving the experience, they shrug their shoulders and say, "That's just the way it is. Games are intense, and I want my child to do well. I feel stressed, but I can keep my cool and stay positive." You can substitute any stressful situation for this baseball game. The problem with this position is that the stress is eating away at them from the inside.

There are two categories of people like Eric: either they're miserable and they fail, or they're miserable and they succeed. It's good to succeed, but the process doesn't have to be as insufferable as sitting on a pack of thumbtacks.

Now let's talk about Jeff. Those who identify with him are not agitated when they face something tough like a game where their child isn't playing well. Somehow, they are much calmer, they believe in themselves, they believe in their child, and they are able to stay supportive and positive. The strikeout, the preparation they have put into their child's game, and the possible embarrassment that their child isn't doing well—none of these factors trigger a negative reaction. They enjoy the game without all the drama. In other words, they accept the conditions as they are and do what they need to do to manage them well. They don't feel stressed.

REACTIONS TO STRESSORS

So here's the important question: what are you doing that causes you to feel so much stress? When your child is sick and you don't know how to help him or her, how do you react? Do you feel fatigued, unqualified, or discouraged? Below is a list of reactions to stress producing situations separated into the three areas of feeling calm, confident, and focused. Write in your journal which reactions best relate to you along with any other reactions that come to mind.

CALM

1. I feel so tense a lot of the time.
2. My stomach is tied up in knots.
3. I'm exhausted most of the time.
4. When my kids don't listen I want to scream.
5. I'm often triggered by things my partner or spouse says or does.

CONFIDENT

1. I don't feel like I'm doing a good job as a parent.
2. I think that others are better parents than I am.
3. I often feel like I don't know what to do in stressful situations.
4. I'm not really up to the job of being a parent.
5. I can't handle really stressful situations.

FOCUS

1. I feel like my efforts as a parent are useless.
2. I feel like I'm putting out fires all the time.
3. I don't have any goals as a parent.
4. I wish my life were different.
5. I don't have faith that things will work out.

As you learn more about basic stress reactions and become more aware of your own frequent stress reactions, you will be able to see when and how you disconnect in your body, mind, and spirit. Then you can begin to use the tools necessary for change.

THE THREE BASIC STRESS REACTIONS

If you suffer from feeling stressed as a parent, you are doing one or more of the following:

- You are holding tension somewhere in your body.
- You are thinking negatively about yourself and how you're doing.
- You are becoming distracted.

Earlier I said that stress is a pressure, strain, or demand. These definitions match up perfectly with the above list. When you grow physically tense, when you think negatively about your performance, or when you are distracted from completing the task at hand, you are putting unnecessary pressure, strain, and demands upon yourself. You know this is happening because you feel like you're being punished or threatened. You may also feel exhausted, uncomfortable, and panicked. The physical tension, the negative thoughts, and the distractions—these are all burdens you are placing on yourself, and they negatively impact your performance. In other words, you are making any situation much harder than it has to be. I call these reactions "disconnecting."

Let's look at the three stress reactions in more detail and at how you are disconnecting from yourself in ways that cause you to feel stressed.

INVOLVEMENT OF BODY, MIND, AND SPIRIT

You are a whole person, one package made up of three interconnected systems: your body, mind, and spirit. That's your team. When you do anything as a parent—clean your house, drive the kids to school, rock your baby to sleep, lay off someone at work, have dinner with your family—all three team members—your body, mind, and spirit—are there performing. Like any winning team, if you want to be successful, each team member has to operate at its very best, and all have to cooperate fully. When your body is calm, your mind confident, and your spirit focused, your team will perform at its best.

DISCONNECTING

The three stress reactions I mentioned earlier in the chapter—physical tension, thinking negatively, and being continually distracted—are the opposite of being calm, confident, and focused. What's more, they have something in common. They all involve pushing away what you need to deal with right now—a messy house, an angry child, a depressed teenager. This is another form of disconnecting. Disconnecting is an important concept that threads through this entire book and is an integral part of my performance model. We are going to focus on what I mean by disconnection and how it causes your stress as a parent.

First, think about the word disconnection. What images come to mind? Here are some that occur to me:

- A telephone line going dead
- Pulling a plug out of a socket
- A head popping off a body
- A wheel flying off a car

The word disconnect is made up of two parts. The Latin origin of *dis* means, "separate, move apart, go in different directions." *Connect* means to "fasten or tie together." So to dis-connect means to pull apart something that is already together. What is the result? Disruption. Disharmony. Disarray. If you're talking on your mobile phone and suddenly you can't hear the other person, the transmission has been disconnected. There is no more communication. If you're reading a book and someone trips over the lamp cord and yanks the plug out of the wall, the light goes out. If you are running the bath water and a pipe outside bursts, the water shuts off. When disconnection takes place out in the world, things cease to function.

This is the same for you. When Joanne's son woke her up in the middle of a peaceful night's rest, because he wet the bed, she was immediately upset. As soon as she became upset, she disconnected from that peace and became stressed. When you disconnect in one of your three "parts"—your body, mind, or your spirit—you are going to feel stressed.

Let's examine each in more detail.

THE BODY

For your body to operate at its best, it needs to be calm. The easiest way to define "calm" is by its opposite: not "tense."

Anna is a good mom. She is loving, kind, and creative. She has taken time to learn good parenting skills including appropriate ways to discipline. She is usually quite successful, but recently when her daughter started screaming because she spilled water on her clothes, Anna froze. Her body became tense. Her heart rate increased, her teeth clenched, and she covered her ears. Her first instinct was to stop the child's screaming by physical force—slapping her mouth or spanking her. Though she refrained from either, she couldn't understand her irrational emotion. She doesn't know what happens to her or why she feels this way, but any time her kids scream her reaction is the same.

While Anna knows she is usually good at discipline, she's not succeeding when it counts—the moment her daughter starts screaming. She's "tense," not calm. When you're tense your muscles are tight or twitchy or your breathing is stopped or irregular, and you feel agitated.

The body is meant to be healthy and whole; relaxed muscles and good, steady breathing are essential to that unity. When we disconnect within our bodies, it means we are losing touch with what's going on inside of us. It's like you've cut out on yourself. You feel stressed out, but you are not aware that you feel that way because you're holding your breath or tensing your muscles. In other words, by disconnecting in your body you are splitting up its wholeness and causing disharmony within the entire system. Why is this stressful? Because when you stop your breath or tense your muscles, you place your body under a strain. Your brain isn't getting the oxygen it needs to survive. Your heart has to pump harder, and you

feel a rush of adrenaline. Glucocorticoids, the chemicals your body man-
ufactures when it's in danger, start coursing through you, putting your
nervous system into a state of excitement. Your body is having a stress
reaction, and whether you are directly conscious of it or not, you feel it.
You may feel "nervous" or "anxious" or like you're having a panic attack.
You might feel an underlying sense of unease, like something's wrong.
These uncomfortable feelings have a physical cause; they originate in the
body. A tense body cannot perform at its best in challenging, stressful,
parenting situations.

In chapter five we will examine how and when you disconnect and
become tense, and you'll learn the three tools for calming down.

THE MIND

For the mind to operate at its best, it needs to be confident. Being confident means believing in yourself. Its opposite is being negative and
self-doubting.

Derek is a new dad. He loves his son but often finds himself discouraged.
*I don't know what I'm doing. Whenever the baby cries I try to comfort him,
but I just can't figure out what he needs. I am so tired all the time because he's
always waking me up. Maybe I'm not cut out to be a father.*

Derek's mind is sabotaging him with negativity.

Mind is a big word. In general, it means the sum total of our consciousness, what we perceive, what we think, and what we believe. One of the
things the mind does is talk to itself in the form of thoughts. It does this a
lot, all the time, in fact. It's like having a talk-radio station on with no "off"
switch. There is a continuous chatter going on inside each one of us, com-
menting on everything we see, think, and feel. "This is green. That's big.
She's funny. He's a jerk. They don't like me. Who cares? I care." and on and
on and on. The commentary also covers what everyone else is doing, but
in this book, we're going to concentrate on how you talk to yourself about
yourself and your parenting capabilities. You are, after all, performing, and

your mind is either your supporter or your critic. It is bringing out the best or the worst in you.

Why is this stressful? When you say to yourself, *I'm not good enough.* and *I will never succeed.* you are disconnecting from your inner support system. In math terms, negative means subtracting, making into a minus, or taking away from. Negative self-statements are no different. They take away your inner support at the moment you most need it in a challenging situation when your capacities should be at their peak. You are disconnecting from the positive side of your mind; you are being disloyal to yourself. You're giving up in the heat of battle, pulling away, and checking out early. What you need at such a time are positive, self-affirming, connecting messages, but you're getting the opposite.

Negative messages are not the truth; they are distortions, because these kinds of statements tend to be global and blown out of proportion. "I'll never succeed. I don't have the patience for this. I'm not a good parent." While there's always room for healthy self-criticism, these overly dramatic statements distort the real picture. They suggest that something is wrong with you, that you are defective, and you might as well give up—none of which would bear up under the evidence. Distortion is one way that we disconnect in our minds. We make grossly negative self-statements; we imagine the worst, and then, of course, we want to bolt.

When you feed yourself negative messages, your mind is working against you instead of helping you. You're under all this pressure to perform with no help from this important system. Your mind is sending out a stream of negative statements and pictures: you see yourself failing miserably; you imagine your child's brain rotting as they veg out on video games; you envision your children are being teased because you didn't buy them the right clothes; you watch your colleagues accept promotions you didn't get because you had to leave early all the time to meet with your daughter's school counselors; you see your husband upset, your children unsatisfied, and you in a loony bin wondering what went wrong. What are most parents afraid of when they're chastising themselves in this way? They're afraid of failure.

When this negative mental process snowballs, it almost guarantees a poor performance, which means that you probably will fail. And this, in turn, sets you up for failing again—a truly vicious cycle.

In chapter six, I will describe in detail how your mind disconnects and becomes embroiled in this dynamic, and I will give you the tools to correct it.

THE SPIRIT

For your spirit to operate at its best, it needs to be focused. "Spirit" is a loaded, often misunderstood word. Depending on your experience it could have negative connotations like being required to attend weekly religious services, or heavy moralizing about what is "good" and "bad." As a performance psychologist, I think of spirit in a different way. In this book, I am speaking about spirit as the part that directs us to become what we're meant to be in life. To me it is the highest self, a person's heart and soul. It's the part that moves me to become a psychologist, my wife a novelist, my college roommate a minister, my next-door neighbor a devoted mother.

Spirit defines and drives us to pursue our authentic goals, and it supports us in taking actions that are consistent with those goals. Simply put, when you are connected in your spirit, then your actions lead you to your goals. When you are disconnected in spirit, you either don't have goals that are important to you, or your actions lead you away from them. A disconnection from the spirit causes people to be distracted:

> Jarod knows he needs to spend time with the kids when he gets home from work. He knows they need his individual attention and love. Every night he comes home thinking about what he needs to do to be a good father but he is tired. His spirit is telling him, "give them attention, help them with their homework, ask them about their day, eat dinner with them, or take them to practice."

But often he keeps working, surfs the web, or just relaxes in front of the TV. His children need him, but he doesn't take the time with them he knows he should. He doesn't know their lives, loves, and fears.

Jarod's spirit is telling him what he needs to do—*I know I should be spending time with the kids*—but Jarod doesn't listen to his spirit and disconnects from it. The result: a poor performance as a parent and so a poor relationship with his children.

Spirit is your driving force. Pay attention and follow through on the direction your spirit is giving you, and you're well on your way to being a successful parent. Disconnect from it, and you get distraction, confusion, disappointment, sub-par performance, and sometimes failure. Your spirit is always directing you to do what's best. When you follow the direction of your spirit, you are focused.

In chapter seven we'll examine your connection to spirit. Are you pursuing goals that are yours or someone else's? Are you staying on track or becoming distracted? Are you staying focused or are you disconnecting?

TEAM "YOU"

Your body, mind, and spirit are your personal team. If any one of them is absent or weak you can't maximize your full potential. But if they work together, each operating at top capacity, you'll hit home runs. Every member of your team must fully participate when you face any challenging situation for you to be in your optimal zone. Any disconnection seriously undermines the whole team's efforts.

Remember this: disconnection in your body, mind, or spirit is the real cause of your stress. If, as a parent, you feel anxious, self-doubtful, or distracted, you are disconnecting in ways that are making you feel that way. The flip side of this is that you can start acting in ways to make you feel calm, confident, and focused. This takes two things: (1) become aware that you are disconnecting; and (2) use specific tools to reconnect. The sooner you become aware that you're disconnecting and the sooner you use the tools to reconnect, the better. Then stress won't have a chance to build, and your performance as a parent will stay steady.

In the next chapter we'll look at where you disconnect, and we'll assess where you need to put more attention, so you don't feel so stressed. Is it your body? mind? spirit? or some combination of all three?

But before that, let's take a short pause for reflection. I've given you a lot of information so far, and I've hit you with two big, heavy concepts: (1) that whatever the conditions of your life as a parent, you are making your life more stressful by how you react; and (2) if you want to make your life more successful, you need to make some changes in how you act. This is the foundation of this book and how I coach people.

If we were meeting in person you might shout at me, "You don't get it Dr. B. I'm stressed out!" So let's establish this right now: I do get it. Life is hard and parenting can be really hard. I coach parents like you on a daily basis. While I nor anyone else cannot save you from whatever you're going through or will go through in your life, I can tell you this: whatever is going on with you, no matter how bad it is, you can turn it around.

There is a big difference between action and reaction. If you feel your life is spiraling out of control, a big reason for it is that chances are you are living in a reactive mode. In your mind the conditions around you (the people, the situations, the circumstances) seem terrible, and you are reacting to them by complaining, shutting down, medicating yourself, or running away. In short, you are disconnecting. I want to strongly encourage you, while you are reading this book, to believe that you can live your life in an active, connected mode. You can take charge of yourself and your parenting. That's what people who live happy, fulfilled lives do. They take charge of their bodies, their minds, and their spirits, and they do what will make them calm, confident, and focused.

If you do what you've always done, you'll get what you've always gotten.

If you want to make some changes in your life, then continue reading and start putting into motion the principles you are learning. Don't waste your time and energy resisting what your spirit guides you to do. This is not about me, the coach, being right. I didn't make up the tools—they come from the best teachers and the most extensive research available in psychology, physiology, and spirituality. What I did was put it all together in one system, so you can benefit from this wisdom now and not have to watch your life as a parent unravel and fall apart and then learn all this stuff.

Truth is truth. I'm your coach. I'm telling you all this stuff because I know this can help you be successful in parenting and in life.

QUESTION & ANSWER

Michelle: We have discussed many new parenting concepts thus far. If we begin to enact the principles we have learned—especially that your stress comes from disconnecting—how will it affect our relationship with our children?

Dr. B: Parenting is a lot about being a model for your children and setting an example for them. In my professional experience, and with rare exception, kids are basically good, and they are just trying to make their way. As a parent you want the best for your kids. They may want something else. How you put that across to them is quite another matter. Your good intentions may end up as screaming matches. If you have a difficult relationship with your child, you may well start to develop a different attitude toward them as you work through this book. I'm not guaranteeing it, since it takes a commitment on their part, too, but changes in a parent's behavior often help to strengthen the parent-child relationship. As you learn to be more calm, confident, and focused in how you parent your children, you'll see that they will begin to recognize that you're making an effort, and might be more willing to meet you halfway. There's no guarantee, of course, but one thing is certain: you'll reduce your own stress level, and that has to have a positive effect on your relationship with your kids.

CHAPTER 4

The Three-Legged Stool

Picture this: your daughter's bedroom is a mess. She's already dashed out of the house to be with her friends after you told her she couldn't go until her room was clean. This isn't happening for the first time. She always does it. And you? Instead of becoming a crazy person (like you usually do), you take a different approach. You take a deep breath and remain calm. You tell yourself you can take care of this. Then you phone or text your child and tell her to come home. Obviously she's mad and embarrassed that you made her leave her pals. All of her problems are suddenly your fault because you told her to clean up her own mess. She's definitely trying to push all your buttons as she stomps back into her room and slams the door. You take another deep breath, remind yourself all this will pass, and you remain lovingly calm and firm. Your child carries on like this from one cutting remark to the next, from one dirty room to the next, from one plea to do it later to the next. You remain a powerhouse of love and consistency.

Do you think this is a fantasy? It's not. Are you saying to yourself, *I can't act like that!*? You can. You just need to learn how.

The secret is reducing the stress in your body, mind, and spirit and to keep your stress at an optimal level throughout each challenge. Think about what throws you off in a parenting situation like the one just described. Do you become hyped up like a jumping bean or stiffen up like a wooden plank? Either way, your body is not calm. You need it to be in a stationary, un-agitated state so you can be reasonable long enough to do what needs to be done. Your mind cannot be undermining you by broadcasting alert warnings. Thoughts like, *I'm the meanest parent on earth!* will not boost your performance. And if you're becoming distracted by thinking, *I'd rather be sitting on a beach in Hawaii than dealing with this child!*, your spirit is deserting you when you need it to help you stay on task and spur you on from start to finish. You have to be the parent and stick with your kids whether you like it or not, and wishing you were someplace else is not the kind of attitude that will pivot your attention toward your goal. In fact, thinking, *I just want this to be over,* only distracts your attention from the task at hand. It increases stress, because it pulls you away from solving the messy bedroom problem or whatever other parenting issue you have to deal with at the moment.

Remember what I said before. Stress is not really caused by what is happening to you from the outside; it comes from the reaction you're having on the inside. The answer to physical tension, negative self-messages, and fractured attention is to learn how to reconnect within yourself. This is how you lower your stress. This is how you stay in the game from start to finish and do your very best, no matter how rough it gets. Whether you are trying to get your child to do his homework, teaching him to be honest, or are concerned about how much money private voice or piano or trumpet lessons will cost, learning to be calm, confident, and focused is key.

If you're thinking, *Is that all there is? If I stay calm, confident, and focused,*

I can be a great parent doing what I have always done? The answer is: of course not. Remember what we said earlier? "If you do what you've always done you will get what you've always gotten." If you go through this process and keep tensing up your body, broadcasting negative messages with your mind, or becoming distracted from your higher goals, you won't perform as the best parent you can be. Even if you find you are strong in one area (calm, confident, or focused) you will want to learn to use all of the tools together to achieve the greatest success, and that will require effort.

Can you be successful in an athletic competition if, when you are getting ready for it, one of your team members doesn't show up at practice? You can't. Teams practice strategic moves together right up until game time. Like them, you can practice training your three team members—your body, mind, and spirit—to work together from the day you start learning to be calm, confident, and focused to the end of every argument or every time you have to discipline your child or any other stressful parenting situation. Success doesn't happen only at the finish line. It's a path. When you're a parent you are on that path, step by step, from beginning to end.

It works like this. Your wife is upset because you travel so much for work. She thinks you should make spending time with the kids and supporting their activities more of a priority—arguing that the kids are, "both of ours; you need to help raise them, too." When she brings up the topic after you return home from a long business trip, you don't want to hear it. You're tired. Your team of three (calm, confident, and focused) are not together. You are calm, for the moment, because you are already breathing deeply, fairly confident you could work things out if you wanted, but entirely unfocused on your wife's concerns. You want to go to bed. The focus member of your team has not yet shown up for practice. So what can you do to be a success in this moment? You need to strengthen your focus by using the focus tools found in chapter seven. Not just in this moment, but every day. By doing this you are on the path to success, and the next time you have an argument with your wife or child your ability to utilize the focus tools will be improved and available to you. Your team will increasingly become stronger, and you will be more prepared to handle even the most unexpected parenting situations.

Your body, mind, and spirit form a natural triad, and a triad is a powerful figure. It's the fundamental structure of harmony in music. In geometry, a three-legged configuration is the sturdiest of structures, much more stable than one that is four-legged. The three-pointed figure always stays a triangle, unlike a square that can be pushed into a parallelogram, or a circle that can be squished into an oval. This unity of three is a potent structure. It shows up in religious traditions and symbols, and it comprises the totality of who you are: body, mind, and spirit.

When I work with parents, I hold up a three-legged stool when I introduce them to the idea that to improve their performance they need a calm body, a confident mind, and a focused spirit. Each leg of the stool represents a different part of you. One leg is your body, one is your mind, and the third is your spirit. Each leg also represents what's necessary to succeed.

Spirit:
Focused

Mind:
Confident

Body:
Calm

The three-legged stool, a structure that is ages old, is one of the most solid, durable, and long-lasting constructions ever produced. In the past, people used it for milking cows and sitting around fireplaces. This configuration forms a three-point foundation that resists toppling. When all three legs of the stool are equally strong, it is remarkably robust; so strong, in fact, that a baby elephant can rest its full weight on it. When your body, mind, and spirit are sturdy and stable, you have a powerful platform on which to build your own optimal performance as a parent. All your parts—your team members—are contributing to the integrity and potentiality of the whole.

Life as a parent is full of unavoidable challenges every day. To meet these challenges successfully, you need a strong foundation. If you were taking a trip across the ocean, you would want a ship that would stand up to a storm. If you are going camping, you want a tent that will stand up to the wind and rain. When you're in the thick of parenting, you want to be sure you can depend on your own internal structure to handle the daily challenges without continually getting stressed out. You need to trust that your "inner team" will be dependable in the face of anything your kids, your partner, or your outside job throws at you. A strong foundation of body, mind, and spirit makes up your three-legged stool. It's a platform that will support you.

But what happens if one of the legs is weak or short? The stool wobbles and loses its stability. Any leg that is weak imposes a strain on the entire system, which places excess pressure on the other two legs. What happens if that baby elephant tries to stand on a stool with one fragile leg? The whole thing collapses, and the elephant falls on its rear end. You operate the same way. You need each leg of your stool to do its job and for all three to be equally strong. If one leg is weak, it will pull the other two down with it.

What does your three-legged stool look like? I have designed a self-diagnostic tool to help you take a snapshot of yours. The Bernstein Performance Inventory (BPI) will give you a reading on which of your legs is the weakest and which is the strongest in challenging and stressful situations. The BPI is made up of nine questions and takes five minutes to complete. By diagnosing yourself, you will find out which leg has been holding you back. You'll identify what your problem area is and where to apply your attention.

THE BERNSTEIN PERFORMANCE INVENTORY (BPI)

Recall a recent parenting situation that was very challenging or stressful for you. It could be anything—stopping your toddler from running into the road, being late for work because your child wouldn't get on the bus, or arguing with your partner because you thought he or she was too lenient or too hard on your teenage son for coming home late.

Visualize the details of the event, remembering the situation as clearly as you can.

What happened and how did you feel about it? In a few words, describe in your journal what the performance situation was:

- My child was in danger and I yelled at her for running in the road.
- My son said he hated school, started crying, sat down, and refused to get on the bus. I had a meltdown because I was late for work.
- My wife yelled at my son and grounded him for a month for coming home late. I disagreed with her discipline and we had a huge argument.

Below are nine statements. Read each one and record in your journal the appropriate number to the right of the statement to indicate how you felt during this performance situation.

Before the Situation Began:

		Not at All	A Little Bit	Somewhat	A lot
1.	I felt calm and relaxed.	0	1	2	3
2.	I was confident in my abilities.	0	1	2	3
3.	I was able to focus on the task.	0	1	2	3

As the Situation Proceeded:

		Not at All	A Little Bit	Somewhat	A lot
4.	I stayed calm the whole time.	0	1	2	3
5.	I remained confident for the duration.	0	1	2	3
6.	I retained my focus all the way through.	0	1	2	3
7.	If I started feeling nervous, I knew how to calm down.	0	1	2	3
8.	If my confidence slipped, I was able to retrieve it.	0	1	2	3
9.	If I lost my focus, I knew how to get back on track.	0	1	2	3

SCORING YOUR BPI

To determine your overall scores, total up your answers as follows:

Calm: Total your answers for questions 1, 4, 7

Confidence: Total your answers for questions 2, 5, 8

Focus: Total your answers for questions 3, 6, 9

After you have added your scores, make a diagram in your journal like the one below and fill in your total scores.

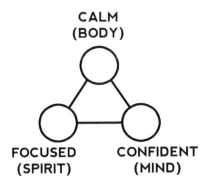

CALM (BODY)

FOCUSED (SPIRIT)

CONFIDENT (MIND)

HOW TO INTERPRET YOUR RESULTS

As you can see, the above diagram looks like a three-legged stool. Examining the numbers in each of the three circles will tell you what your relative strengths and weaknesses are. Since the highest score you can achieve in any one "leg" is nine, any number less than nine shows that you need to reinforce that leg.

To show you how scores are interpreted and where you can go from there, let me walk you through the example.

Karen, a busy mother of four, is struggling with her seven-year-old's incessant crying. Karen's BPI scores: Calm—4; Confident—6; Focused—8.

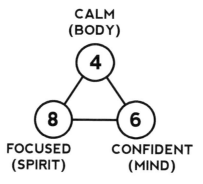

What do these numbers tell us about Karen? Obviously, her strongest leg is Focus, her weakest is Calm, and Confident is somewhere in between. After listening to Karen tell her own story about how she approaches her daughter's tears, her BPI scores will make sense to you:

> I might not be the most patient parent, but in general I'm a pretty good mom. I am involved in my children's lives. I make sure they eat well, go to bed on time, and I give them lots of hugs and kisses—when they let me. Lately, I've been putting forth an extra bit of effort each day to stay calm with my kids. Today, Emily, my seven-year-old, pushed every button I had and even the ones I didn't know existed. I was helping her memorize the notes of the

musical scale. We've been working on this for months—the same notes on the same scale. She practices her piano pieces, but she refuses to memorize the notes on the scale. I was insistent that she learn the notes and assured her that I would help her. She began to sob crocodile tears—enough to fill a small swamp. Her eyes got puffy and her face blotchy. This isn't a rare occurrence. It happens daily over all sorts of things. The louder and harder she cried, the more upset my other kids became, simply adding to the chaos.

I told Emily she shouldn't be crying, I should, and I almost did. My shoulders were tense; I didn't know what to do. When I tried to stay calm she cried harder, when I became upset she cried harder. Either way she cried harder. I tried different approaches, reasoning, love, and discipline. She cried harder and harder and harder. My teeth were clenched, my heart beat faster, and I could feel my body temperature rise. I just wanted to throw my hands in the air, cut my losses, and run out of the room screaming. This one instance affected my entire morning and afternoon. I was tense, tired, and discouraged. I don't want to feel like this, and I know this isn't the best outcome, but I just don't know what to do. Everything I tried failed.

Karen's Focus score was 8 out of a possible 9. That's to be expected since she reported that she stayed engaged with the challenge. When something didn't work, she tried something else. That means she was connected to her spirit, her driving force, and had no trouble staying on track. Karen's Confidence score, at 6, was shakier. She was, from time to time, beset by negative thinking that undermined her belief in her abilities. She felt like she didn't know what to do, and she was becoming discouraged and thinking negatively about her daughter and herself.

Karen's inability to stay calm in the face of impending tears was her weakest leg. Her score of 4 in the Calm leg attests to her difficulties. From her own words, we can tell that she was dissociating from her body, which caused her to become more and more physically tense, which in turn made her feel ungrounded. Naturally, the fact that Karen's heart was pounding and she had trouble breathing became a significant distraction. It made it harder to keep connecting to the task at hand. This, in turn, affected her confidence. As her confidence level slipped, she found it harder to rebound.

What we see from this example is how the weakness in one leg—Calm—put a physical strain on the entire structure and kept Karen from achieving the happy outcome she hoped for, considering how hard she tried. Had she been able to remain calm, physically—keeping her jaw open, heart rate lower, shoulders relaxed, and body temperature regular—she would have had a much different experience all together.

Karen's strongest leg was her ability to stay focused on a goal, so I gave her a new goal to focus on: to learn to become calm in the face of her daughter's unreasonable crocodile tears. In no time at all, Karen learned the three tools for calming down and used them on a daily basis. As she learned to dissolve her physical tension before it mounted and threw her off, we noticed that Karen's ability to focus grew even stronger than it had been before. She was able to maintain control of her body by staying calm.

Once Karen had calmed down, she was able to focus on the problem rather than the symptom. She realized that Emily's crying had little to do with memorizing notes on the scale and came from a much deeper issue—Karen and her husband's marital relationship was struggling. Arguing, tension, and anger filled their home night and day. Emily felt the stress of it, and she didn't know how to channel her emotions, so she would just cry. Being calm, instead of getting angry, allowed Karen to have perspective of what was causing Emily to cry so often. Naturally, this gave Karen's confidence a huge boost because she now knew what was causing Emily's emotional outbursts, and she had a new direction to pursue in helping Emily. She held Emily and said, "I realize that it's hard for you when Daddy and I are fighting. We have some things to work out, and we're doing just that." Karen grew ever more sure of herself as she was able to respond to

Emily in similar situations without her own physical tension overwhelming her.

Remember: working on any one of the legs immediately links you to the other two and makes your whole system stronger.

YOUR SCORES GIVE YOU A STARTING POINT

Reflect on your BPI scores. What does your three-legged stool look like? Which is your strongest leg? Which is your weakest? Remember: you are not comparing yourself to anyone else—just to yourself. These scores tell you what you need to strengthen in order to reduce your stress and improve your performance as a parent.

As you do this you may be thinking, *Hey, wait a minute, Dr. B! My BPI scores aren't accurate. They say that I'm not very confident. But that's not true! I'm usually very sure of myself.*

The BPI is not a definitive statement on how you are in every aspect of your life. It is meant to help you examine how you handle challenges and perform under pressure. Take a few moments to consider whether your BPI scores accurately represent how you are in most stressful parenting situations. Sometimes when people take the BPI, the situation that comes to mind is a horror story and how they responded in a way that isn't really typical of their usual performance. Consequently, their BPI scores aren't representative of how they react to most stressful situations. Look at your scores, and ask yourself if they are a reflection of how you perform most of the time in stressful situations. If you find that your BPI scores don't reflect your usual performance under stress, then retake the inventory based on what you are usually like in stressful situations to obtain a more accurate general reading.

Before we go on, look at your scores again. What do you most need to strengthen? Being calm? Remaining confident? Or staying focused?

In the next three chapters, we will take on each leg of the stool. You can begin by working on your shortest leg (your lowest score) by going straight to the chapter that addresses it. Or, you can start with your strongest score—some people benefit the most by working from their strength. While I recommend that you read sequentially through the next three core chapters, this model is not a rigid structure that you have to squeeze yourself into. Its beauty is that wherever you begin, you will end up encompassing the whole. Even if you scored high in one particular leg, it's still important to check out the tools in that chapter, because you can always grow stronger. If you happened to score low on all three, that is only showing you that you have room to grow in all three areas.

The end goal of this book is to teach you to become calm, confident, and focused as you live your life as a parent, facing all the many challenges you have to face, whether it's overwhelming piles of laundry, honey-do lists that never end, late nights wondering what your teenager is doing, or working towards a better relationship with your spouse. When you know how to become calm, confident, and focused you will always have a sturdy, secure foundation and be ready to perform at your best and be a success at being yourself.

IT'S ALL ABOUT STAYING CONNECTED

I'll sum up this chapter by saying this: if you want to succeed you have to stay connected in your body, mind, and spirit. Since being disconnected means being separated from the whole, being disconnected inside of you means that the body, mind, and spirit are detached from one another. It can also mean that there is a disconnection within any one or more of the three systems.

To put it more simply, when you find yourself in a tough spot—whining kids and no energy to cook, a business trip that overlaps your son's choir concert, or worrying that your daughter is experimenting with drugs—maybe you tense up. Maybe you become afraid and tell yourself you can't handle it. Maybe you find it impossible to keep your mind on what's in front of you right now. You want to escape and check out early. This is disconnecting. It has a purpose. It is a way of coping with a difficult situation.

But remember what I said in the first chapter: If you want to accomplish your goals—goals that are important and will make a valuable contribution to your life and to the lives of your children—you have to be present. Sure, you can bail and run away, but that only postpones the inevitable. At some time you're going to have to face whatever difficult situation you are avoiding. Really be there. The challenge—whether it's at home with the kids or in your office at work—isn't going to go away. Disconnecting from yourself in a vain attempt to disappear in spirit, even if you can't physically remove yourself, doesn't work. The more you disconnect, the higher your stress will be. You're going to feel worse and worse, and your performance as a parent will suffer.

In the next three chapters, I'm going to give you the tools to stay connected in each member of your "team"—your body, mind, and spirit. You'll be happy to know that there are only nine tools, three for each team member. The tools are simple, intuitive, and have been around for hundreds, if not thousands, of years. Parents have always been on a quest to be more calm, confident, and focused. And those who use the tools succeed. Just as you will.

CULTIVATING NEW HABITS

Notice that I just said, "Those who use the tools succeed." Why am I underscoring this point?

If the doctor gave you a prescription to cure your flu, and you taped the prescription to your bathroom mirror and never took it to the pharmacist, or if the pharmacist filled the prescription but you never took the medication, nothing would happen. No change. That's how it is with the tools I am going to give you. They will sit on the page, like the prescription taped to the mirror, until you do something with them.

Unless you're actively involved in the process of using what's in this book, your parenting experience will remain unchanged. You have to take what I'm offering and not just think about it—an important first step—you have to use it. I can tell you, from many years of experience, that this is hard for most people. Why? Because we generally prefer to hang out on the couch and hit the remote rather than get up and take action. What's more, in this process you have to be willing to look at yourself clearly and honestly, which is also a real challenge for most people. Unless you want to make some changes in how you think and act, and unless you actually make those changes, everything will stay the same.

The change I am talking about is in reference to your habits. Like everyone else, you have habits in dealing with life's situations—particularly the stressful ones.

Rather than labeling your parenting habits "good" or "bad," let's call them "productive" and "unproductive." A productive habit is an action or series of actions that leads to growth. It is a habit that creates success, and it doesn't hurt you or anyone else. In fact, it has potential benefits for you and others. Telling your children you love them every day would be a productive habit. Unproductive habits create strife and disappointment and don't lead anywhere. They keep you stuck and may be harmful to you or your children. For example, spending more of your free time with your friends than with your children would be an unproductive habit if your goal were to be a better parent. What are your productive habits? How can you transform your unproductive habits to become productive?

Given our definition of stress as a function of disconnection, and that disconnection leads to poor performance, we are looking to build productive habits: habits that keep you connected, habits that build a better you as a parent and a better environment for that parenting to take place.

Back to the seed packet analogy: a productive habit would be one that tends the plant and helps it grow, so that it can eventually blossom and flower. The productive habit would look like this: watering the garden, weeding it, fertilizing it, and being patient. An unproductive habit would be attending to the plant haphazardly or neglecting it entirely, thinking someone else will take care of it.

Productive habits are ones that connect; unproductive habits disconnect. A productive habit produces a positive result; an unproductive habit produces a negative result. In terms of our model of the three-legged stool, productive habits keep you calm, confident, and focused. Productive habits keep stress at an optimal level. Unproductive habits produce more stress. Your unproductive habits keep you anxious, self-doubting, and distracted. They keep you stressed out.

As a parent making sure to have dinner with your family each night could be considered a productive habit. It gives you time to connect to your children, laugh with them, and take a peek at some of the things they struggle with. This is a habit that keeps you informed and confident with your children, as well as focused. That little bit of down time can help you feel calmer when things are hard. On the flip side spending hours each night watching TV could be considered an unproductive habit. It can easily keep you from engaging with your children, add to your anxiety because you are going against what your spirit is telling you—which is to spend time with the kids, eat dinner with them, go to their game, and help them with homework. This unproductive habit may cause the feeling of self-doubt, feeling like you are a bad parent because you are not acting as a parent. You are watching TV.

We are creatures of habit. All of us. Our lives are shaped by our habits: habits of action (walking, talking, eating); habits of thinking (things we like, things we don't like); and habits of feeling (what makes us happy, sad, or angry). Habits are a series of learned actions, which we repeat in sequence. We need habits because without them, any action we perform would be as if for the first time. Take the habit of walking into a darkened room and turning on a light. When you cross the threshold into that room you are in the habit of reaching to your right for a light switch. Then, you're in the habit of flipping it on. Imagine if you didn't have that habit. Every time you walked into a darkened room, you wouldn't know what to do. You'd stay in the dark. Habits provide patterns and give structure to our lives. They also have a lot to do with how well or poorly we handle stress and how well or poorly we perform as a parent.

The tools of being calm, confident, and focused are the building blocks of all productive habits. Remember, your personal team has three members: your body, mind, and spirit. Each one can have productive or unproductive habits. Ultimately, it's your choice which habits you want to cultivate.

I've often worked with parents who want their children to be calm, confident, and focused, but they themselves are not. In other words, the parents don't "walk their talk." The parent is sending the child a confusing message ("I want you to be one way, but it's OK if I'm not."). The subtler and no less confusing message is, "I want you to love and respect me as your parent regardless of how I am, but you need to do as I say to gain my love and respect." In using the tools you can actively clear up any confusion your child has as to who you are. When you start cultivating productive parenting habits now, you'll be a better example to your children. You'll know how to turn on the light and dispel the darkness.

QUESTION & ANSWER

Michelle: Dr. B, I have done the BPI test on myself numerous times. Depending on the situation my scores vary. Sometimes I'm very confident but not calm. Sometimes I'm very calm but not focused. Sometimes I'm very focused but not confident. Is this normal or am I doing something wrong?

Dr. B: Using the BPI for different situations is an excellent practice. Remember, your body, mind, and spirit are in a fluid, dynamic relationship with one another. As the outer conditions change—your child is in trouble; your partner is having a meltdown; the bank is bouncing your checks—your "inner" response will shift. At any one time you may feel more physically tense or more self-doubtful or more distracted. Using the BPI to reflect on different situations will help sharpen your awareness of how you are reacting in stress-producing situations. When are you disconnected? And where—in your body, mind, or spirit?

Refining your awareness can only be helpful, because it will lead you directly to know which tools to use to reduce your stress and keep it at an optimal level. You're not doing anything wrong! Quite the contrary, cultivating your awareness through using the BPI will help you to be more proactive by anticipating stress-producing events, so you can use the necessary tools to maintain your connection.

CHAPTER 5

How to Calm Down

When you are performing as a parent, your body is in the room and engaged whether you realize it or not. In this chapter we'll look at what's going on with your body in stressful situations and how you can practice staying calm to reduce your stress.

Linda was concerned about her teenage daughter's depression and came to me for help. "I feel awful," she said. "My daughter is making me crazy! She is negative about everything, and she won't participate in anything. Whenever I try to help her she tells me to go away. I don't know what to do."

I asked Linda to close her eyes and imagine the scene at home with her daughter. "Tell me what you're seeing," I said.

Linda closed her eyes and began. "As soon as my daughter gets home from school she goes straight to her bedroom. I try to talk to her, but she yells at me to go away. She won't give me any information, so I talk to her teachers and friends. I just want to help but then she accuses me of messing with her business. She won't open up to me at all. I guess she just doesn't trust me."

As Linda was speaking there was a whole other scenario going on with her body that I observed and of which she was unaware. Her shoulders tensed up, her brow became deeply furrowed, her breathing sped up, and her hands clenched tightly. "I get so frustrated!" she said, with deep emotion. I told her to freeze and open her eyes to look at what was going on with her body. I then asked Linda if she thought her difficulties with her daughter had anything to do with how much tension she was adding to the scene? "No!" Linda said. "My daughter is making me tense."

From Linda's point of view, it was her daughter's depression and defiance that were causing her stress. However, Linda's daughter didn't cause her tension. What's more, Linda was anxious about her daughter being self-destructive. But it wasn't simply her thoughts that made her anxious. All of the tense and anxious things Linda was doing with her body were creating her anxiety: tensing her shoulders, clenching her fists, breathing faster, and furrowing her brow. Her actions intensified her anxious feelings and thoughts.

Tensing your body causes stress. Adrenaline surges through your gut, your blood pressure shoots up, and your entire system goes on alert. A torrent of stress hormones is unleashed into your bloodstream, and it becomes increasingly hard to focus and think. It may seem like your child's depression and defiance are causing your tension, but really they are just words and thoughts coming from someone's mouth and mood. They aren't doing anything *to* you. Your stress is mounting and your performance is suffering because *you* are disconnecting from your own body. You are not aware of what your body is doing, but it's spinning out of control. Remember: disconnection causes stress and too much stress causes poor performance.

It's the same for any type of performance. If a soccer player is sitting on the bench waiting to go into the game and she keeps tensing her body, when the coach finally sends her out on the field she will be nervous right from the start. She'll miss shots she ought to be making, and she'll be out of sync with her teammates. It doesn't matter how hard she practiced. She needs to stay loose on and off the field. If a pianist's fingers lock in the middle of a piece, they can't float effortlessly over the keys. Again, it doesn't matter how well he knows the music. If a mother goes into an argument with her daughter already tense with clenched fists and a tight jaw, she will not perform well.

In all these cases, the individuals are disconnected from their bodies. Remember the three-legged stool? Disconnection in one leg immediately hobbles the other two. When you lose the feeling of calm in your body, it precipitates negative thoughts (in your mind), and you'll easily become distracted and lose heart (in your spirit). Stress can build very rapidly, and when it grows past a certain point, your performance will suffer. Guaranteed.

To improve your performance as a parent you have to learn to reduce the stress in your body. When you have to do anything—work late, deal with your depressed teenager, or discuss the glaring C-minus on your child's report card—you want your body to be calm. I realize that "calm" and "parenting" might sometimes seem like a contradiction in terms. In your parenting years you are often filled with lots of worry, drained of energy, and stretched beyond capacity. While all that is true, learning how to calm yourself down is a necessary and invaluable skill that will only improve such situations.

AWARENESS FIRST

To get your body into a calmer state you need to learn two things:

1. How to recognize when you are not calm, and
2. How to use specific tools to calm yourself down.

If you're like most people, you are probably not very aware of your body throughout the day, unless you're in pain or you feel sick. A sore throat, a stomach ache, a cold, a fever, and a tooth ache call attention to themselves. But until the discomfort reaches an uncomfortable level, we tend to minimize or even ignore the early signs. It's nothing. It will go away. We don't become aware until the pain is virtually shouting at us. My tooth is killing me! That's when we do something about it.

For certain people this doesn't hold true—people who use their bodies all the time—like dancers, swimmers, or singers. They have to pay close attention, not ignore any signs that all is not well, and attend to them because their jobs depend on it—as they often perform in front of a crowd. The upside is that they are connected to what goes on in their bodies. Most of us don't have that threat hanging over us. The problem we have is that when we ignore the signs of disconnection, it causes stress to build. But ultimately, we face the same failure. It behooves us to increase our body awareness—when we are not calm—so we know how to deal with it at critical times.

Let's start with this question: what signs and symptoms in your body tell you that you are not calm?

I know when I'm not calm because . . .

(Which apply to you?)

- My chest feels tight.
- I have a headache or feel one coming on.
- My shoulders ache.
- My neck feels stiff.
- I stop breathing.
- My stomach hurts.
- My heart beats rapidly.
- I clench my teeth.
- My muscles ache.
- I start sweating.
- My skin feels prickly.

- I feel tense all over.
- I feel like I'm gasping for air.
- My feet curl up.
- My legs cramp.
- I make fists with my hands.
- I feel like I want to run away.
- My mind starts racing.
- I start talking too fast.
- I bite my nails.
- My nerves are jittery.
- My eyes ache.
- My voice rises.
- I feel generally uncomfortable.

Perhaps you identified with one, perhaps ten. Everyone is different, so consider what other symptoms may be true for you.

People often ask me, "But why is it necessary to be aware first?" Think about it this way. When you are driving a car and you see a sign that says STOP, it is telling you exactly what you need to do: put your foot on the brake, and stop the car. If you disregard the sign and keep going, you are risking your own life and that of others. The physical signs of tension in your body are like a stop sign sending you a message. It is your body's way of signaling to you that you are disconnected, which is useful to know because it tells you that you need to reconnect to your body and calm down. If you don't pay attention to these signs, you are going to crash.

Awareness of when you are not calm is the first step in the process of reconnecting with your body.

REFINING YOUR AWARENESS

It doesn't matter how many or how few items you checked above. Becoming aware of what is going on with your body when you are not calm is a big step in the right direction. Besides, there are only three basic ways we human beings lose our sense of calm. Each of your responses on the checklist is related to one of these:

1. We stop breathing or we breathe irregularly.
2. We become ungrounded.
3. We shut down in one or more of our five senses.

Before moving on to the three tools for calming down, I would like you to cultivate your awareness of how and when you disconnect from the calm leg of your three-legged stool. Does something go awry with your breath? Do you lose touch with the floor under you? Do your muscles get tense? Do you stop seeing (or hearing) clearly?

Read through the chart below and think about the questions it's asking you, then answer what you can. If you can't answer all of the questions right now that's fine. You might need to do some self-observation first, so you can collect what us psychologists call "baseline data" on yourself. Record your observations in your journal.

Remember, the more you cultivate your awareness of the ways in which you disconnect from your body, the more quickly you will be able to catch the stress well before it builds. In other words, you will reconnect right away and actually reduce the stress. It won't have a chance to reach the point of having a negative impact on your performance. Even better, it will be at just the right level (remember the stress/performance curve on page 16) so that you can perform at your best.

As you consider the chart, remember a stressful parenting situation you recently faced or imagine you are about to engage in one.

AWARENESS INVENTORY: BODY

When I am in a situation that I feel is stressful, I notice the following things in my body:

In each category, which apply to you?

Breathing	• I hold my breath. • My breathing becomes very shallow. • I breathe erratically (I gasp, I stop breathing, I take small breaths).
Grounding	• I'm not aware of the floor or of the chair I'm sitting on. • My feet are coming off of the ground. • I feel tension in my (name body parts).
Sensing	• I tend to close down (i.e. I'm not aware of) these senses: touch, smell, taste, sight, hearing.

As you recall or experience overwhelming parenting situations, you may realize that you are doing all sorts of unhelpful things with your body that you probably didn't notice before. The difference now is that you are going to pay attention and treat the symptoms in your body as road signs to help you stop and reconnect. The more aware you are, the more effectively you can use the tools.

THE THREE TOOLS FOR CALMING DOWN

Now you are ready to learn the three tools for calming down. These tools will help you to quickly reduce any stress building up in your body. The tools are easy to learn and effective.

TOOL #1: CALMING DOWN BY BREATHING

It should come as no surprise that breathing is the first tool. Let's work on this together.

- Take a good deep breath. Inhale . . . breathe in through your nose.
- Exhale . . . breathe out through your mouth.
- Do it again . . . inhale . . . exhale.

Notice where your breath is going. When I ask people to "take a good deep breath" almost everyone puffs up their lungs and upper chest. This is not a deep breath. A breath that raises your shoulders and expands your chest does not calm you down; it actually amps you up. I call it a "fight or flight breath" because it prepares you to do battle or to run away. This kind of breathing feels like fear. It's what the body does when it's reacting to danger.

Imagine you are walking in a jungle and suddenly a venomous snake is coiled in front of you, hissing and ready to strike. Fear courses through your body. When you take a big gulp of air while facing a deadly snake, it goes to your upper chest. Either you're going to face the danger, or you're going to run away from it. Either way, this is a survival breath, and its purpose is not to relax you. A calming breath, on the other hand, goes to a different and deeper place—your belly, which is why the first tool is a calming belly breath.

A young mother shares an experience she had with one of her children:

> As I was in the bathroom getting myself ready for the day, and my two youngest kids were sitting and playing on the floor. I admit I was more concerned about the curl in my hair than their quiet playfulness, until they showed me their lovely artwork—all over the new bathroom tile we had just installed. My first breath was one quick chest-raising gasp. Not relaxing in any way. My first words were sharp and angry, and my body was tense, ready for a fight. As I quickly became aware of myself—my quick breathing, and furrowed brow—I took a deep calming breath, and almost immediately I had more control of myself. I also had a better outlook on my children's innocence, and became more thoughtful of my lack of supervision over them. I took another deep belly breath and focused on what I wanted to teach them. I was now able to act instead of react. I was able to be successful in that moment as a parent simply because I changed the way I was breathing.

Let's work on taking a deep, calming breath.

EXERCISE:
THE BELLY BREATH

To begin, sit comfortably in a chair with your back well supported.

Place your body in an open position—uncross your arms and your legs. (If your arms or legs are crisscrossed you will restrict your airflow.)

Rest your palms on your thighs and place both feet on the floor.

Now place your hands on top of your navel and let your belly just relax. This means don't hold your belly in. (Resist any temptation here to suck in your stomach so you can look thin.) Let your belly hang out and relax. First, exhale through your mouth . . . now breathe in through your nose, but don't suck in your belly. Let it stay expanded. You will feel the breath seep into your lungs as you breathe in, but your chest won't be heaving up and down. Both belly and chest will be calm as your breath keeps dropping down into your lower belly.

Slowly, breathe in and out three times in this open, expanded position, chest relaxed and belly wide.

If you want to deepen your breath even more, reach your hands around you and place your palm and fingers on both sides of your lower back right along the hips. Now, breathe deeply down and feel your bottom back ribs very gently expand as you do this. This is a small, subtle movement. You have to be quiet and tuned in to feel it, but as you sense this gentle movement of your ribs you will notice your calmness deepening.

Now, inhale again, deeply down into your belly and lower back. Slowly exhale . . . let the breath out gently.

Breathe in and out like this three times.
Feel yourself calming down. Don't force the breath in and out
 and don't hyperventilate.

At this point you might start yawning or feel sleepy. Many people have this reaction. Recently, an overworked father came to me for some coaching on his parenting skills. As he talked about himself and his children he barely paused for a breath. He ran through an incredibly long list of responsibilities and burdens he carried. We started working on deepening and regularizing his breath. In less than five minutes he started yawning. A lot. Then he actually started falling asleep! His system was so tightly wound and deprived of oxygen, so needing to rest, that given the first opportunity to calm down he almost conked out. So, if you are yawning, are sleepy, or feel lightheaded as you start paying attention to and deepening your breath, know that this is actually a good sign. Your body is calming down. It is telling you that it is not used to breathing deeply and regularly, and it needs some rest!

The way to deep belly breathing is to work slowly, gently, and determinedly on cultivating your breath. It may feel a little strange at first and all that oxygen might make you feel a bit lightheaded. Your system simply isn't used to taking real breaths. It's used to short, choppy, mini breaths. After a while though, deep, steady breathing will feel like the most natural, calming thing in the world.

IRREGULAR BREATHING

The most frequent way we disconnect from our bodies is by holding our breath or breathing irregularly.

When I observe parents in stressful situations, I see this familiar scenario: Their children yell at them, and then you hear a quick breathe and then silence. They are holding their breath.

Why is this significant? Because holding your breath immediately causes stress. Without breath your brain is deprived of oxygen. It starts sounding an alarm: YOU ARE DYING! This is a fact: if your brain really were cut off from oxygen permanently, you would die. The automatic reaction to a loss of oxygen broadcasts an emergency signal. This isn't conscious. It's instinctive. Your anxiety level is directly affected by how you breathe. Stop breathing, and your anxiety level immediately shoots up.

But there is another connection between your breath and your ability to think clearly and logically when in a stressful situation. Breath is intimately connected to your thinking. A shortage of breath causes a fear reaction, which disturbs an orderly thought process.

When your breath has stopped or it is irregular, chances are that your thoughts are jumping around, and you are worrying about the future (What's going to happen . . . ?), or you are dwelling on the past (If only I had . . .). When your breath is steady and regular and you are able to be in the present moment, then your brain is free to deal with the task at hand. Conscious attention to the breath puts you firmly here, now. And that's just where you have to be when you're a parent. You must deal with the issue in front of you, right now. It doesn't matter what you did yesterday (past) or what you're going to do tomorrow (future), you have to think and act now, in the present. This is hard to do if your thinking is restless, if you're anxious about what's going to happen, or if you're endlessly replaying what already went wrong. The remedy to this situation is not mind control. It's breath control. With regular, steady breathing, you can be in the present and give your full attention to the question in front of you. Your thinking will be clearer.

> James had reached his maximum patience level with his 'tween daughter. She was never happy and always complaining. If she had to wash dishes, there were complaints. If she had to do her homework, more complaints. If she had to eat dinner—which her parents took great effort and time into making healthy and

enjoyable—she complained. One evening, while helping her finish a science project, James was momentarily sidetracked by the baby's crying. This upset his daughter, and she began complaining that no one was helping her.

His daughter's sour attitude immediately triggered a negative reaction in him. He gave off a big huff and then a giant puff and it looked like a blast of steam was coming out of his head. His fists clenched, his shoulders hunched, his breathing became erratic. His mind became fogged and all he could see or hear were her complaints. He was no longer in the moment but in the past, re-living every ungrateful moment and every complaint she had ever made. The more he relived the past, the faster and shorter his breathing became, and the more he lost himself in the fog of his mind. He was at a crossroads of success and failure in dealing with his daughter's negativity, and failure was closely looming.

Just as he began to release his anger, he became aware that his fists were clenched and his teeth were grinding. He removed himself from the situation, and in another room took three deep belly breaths. As his breathing slowed he was able to return to the present with a clear mind. He went back, apologized for allowing himself to be so easily triggered, and finished helping his daughter with her project.

While James and his daughter worked together, he took the opportunity to talk with her about how her complaining affected him, her, and the rest of the family. He pointed out to his daughter that though he did get upset, he was able to become aware of his body and manage his stress, in the moment, by breathing. He also suggested that the next time she became upset, she would benefit from some deep belly breathing.

This had a much better outcome than blowing off steam. His daughter felt loved, learned that her complaining had a negative impact on everyone including herself, and began to notice and feel gratitude for the support she had received from her father. She also learned, from her father's example, how to reduce her own stress when she was upset. Deep breathing made all the difference. Though his daughter continued to complain at times, this father had learned how to stay calm, even when his daughter complained ('tweens are 'tweens, after all!).

PUTTING BREATHING INTO ACTION

The next time you notice that you are not calm, treat the anxious feelings like a road sign. If your stomach is churning, or you start sweating, or your legs are shaking, your body is sending you a message: "You need to calm down." This is your awareness kicking in. The first thing to ask yourself is, *How am I breathing?* because it is the most primary question. You've probably stopped breathing or your breathing has become very shallow or irregular. Do the exercise above, and you will feel yourself calming down immediately.

Once you have started breathing deeply and regularly, say "thank you" inside. Why do this? Because the awareness you just received that you were not breathing is a gift. It is a realization to be grateful for. Whether you believe your awareness comes from a God, a Goddess, a Higher Power, your Highest Self, Nature, the Universe, or Life, the very fact that it is coming to you at all is like a present. Gratitude acknowledges the giver and encourages future giving. Imagine receiving a wonderful gift from someone and not saying thank you. The giver wouldn't feel like being generous again, "Well, she didn't say 'Thank you' last time." Expressing gratitude invites more of what you're grateful for to come your way.

What most people do when they notice that they are "breathing wrong" is to beat themselves up—*I can't believe I'm still doing that! When am I gonna learn?* They don't appreciate the awareness at all. This kind of critical response is not allowed! I urge you to try saying "thank you" every time you become aware of anything that you are trying to change in yourself. Gratitude is the opposite of criticism, and it spreads an atmosphere of kindness and compassion—exactly the right atmosphere for inner growth.

As Linda and Burt struggled to put their very sick three-year-old son, Sam, to bed, stress was high. It was supposed to be their date night. For the whole week previously, they had hardly spent any time together, and they were excited for the evening. To their disappointment however, their night out had to be postponed because Sam was sick. In hopes of still enjoying their time together they planned to watch a movie on their own comfy couch.

Just as they were sitting down with their popcorn, Sam threw up all over the chair and carpet—it was going to be a long night. Burt cleaned up the chair and started to wash the carpet while Linda cleaned up Sam and herself. Once purged of the puke they sat down together, started their movie and despite efforts to keep the regurgitation in a bowl they once again found themselves covered in sliminess and off to the showers and laundry room. They were already exhausted before the evening began, and now they were extra tired of cleaning up the throw up.

Burt was especially frustrated and began to be upset. It was the usual muscle tightening, furrowed brow, accompanied by a headache. But just as his frustration started to mount he became aware of his body. Because of this awareness, he took a moment to breathe and could quickly see the situation for what it was. He gave a big inner "thank you" for becoming aware. He really was grateful, because this awareness kept him from saying and doing things that would have made him feel bad or simply just made the evening harder. Instead this small drop of gratitude to himself created a stream of gratitude: thankfulness that he was a dad, that he could help his son, and that he could do all of this with his wife by his side. His love and compassion soared. No doubt it was a long night for them, but instead of stressing they were able to get through the evening with a positive attitude.

Breathing deeply and then saying "thank you" reduces feelings of stress, and you actually improve the possibility of attaining your goals because you are cultivating a helpful relationship with the powers of change. When you breathe deeply and regularly, you are giving your brain, blood, and body the oxygen it needs to perform optimally. Even if you don't believe in a God, Goddess, or Higher Power, expressing gratitude still cultivates a better relationship with your own consciousness and highest self (the best person you can be).

TOOL #2: CALMING DOWN BY GROUNDING

Erin is at the doctor's office with her son Jake who is having recurring migraines. They are waiting for results to come back from the MRI scan and are imagining the worst. She and her son are fidgety and their anxiety is mounting. Erin is perched on the edge of her chair, one foot coiled around the leg. Her other foot is lifting off of the ground, knee and leg bouncing. She is definitely not calm. What's wrong with this picture? Erin is very ungrounded.

When we lose awareness of and contact with the ground we disconnect in our bodies, and this triggers anxiety and tension.

There is a great, settling, connecting force on earth and it's called gravity. Gravity holds us to the earth and keeps everything from spinning away and out of control. We've all seen the pictures of astronauts floating around. They're in a zero-gravity environment. It looks like fun, but here on earth, it would make us feel shaky and tenuous. We feel most secure when we are in contact with the earth, and we become ungrounded when we pull away from the earth, often without even realizing it.

When I find myself deep in thought about some challenge—say I'm about to talk to an audience of a thousand people—my thoughts may become anxious, I should have prepared more. Maybe I won't remember everything I have to say. Am I going to start sweating? Will they like me? I begin to notice that I am definitely not feeling the chair I'm sitting on, nor am I feeling the floor under my feet. This is what I mean by "becoming ungrounded."

Why is this noteworthy? When I'm ungrounded, I literally lose touch with the ground. I'm running away from the present moment. When I pull my awareness back into the present, however, I feel the chair supporting me. When I consciously place my feet squarely on the floor, I feel that supporting me too. Immediately the anxiety lessens, even though the situation hasn't changed. I am still about to speak to a large group of people, but my attitude toward it has changed. I have physically reconnected to where I am right now and what I have to do now. Grounding, quite simply, has a profound calming effect on the body and mind, giving you an enhanced ability to fulfill your spirit and perform.

Becoming grounded has two parts. The first part is what we have just discussed, feeling supported by the floor and the chair.

To have this experience, do the following simple exercise as you continue reading:

 ## EXERCISE:
GROUNDING YOURSELF

Start by sitting comfortably, upright, in a chair.
Uncross your arms and your legs.
Place your feet flat on the floor.
Breathe down to your belly.
Now, feel the floor under your feet.
Feel the floor supporting your feet.
Now feel your body sitting on the chair.

Feel your legs and butt and back touching the chair. If the chair
has arm rests, feel your arms being supported by them.
Feel your whole body being supported by the floor and the
chair.

This is the first part of grounding. Continue the exercise for one minute
and enjoy the calm feeling that comes over you.

Did you remember to breathe? Most people, when they start learning
how to ground themselves, often stop breathing! Don't let that happen. You
can use two tools simultaneously just by keeping your breathing deep and
steady as you ground yourself by feeling the support of the floor and chair.

The combination of breathing and grounding is very powerful and goes
a long way toward connecting you to your own body, calming yourself
down, and staying present.

The second part of grounding is letting go of physical tension. Let's look
at Erin again. As she waits for her sons test results her shoulders are hiked
way up, her brow is deeply furrowed, and her chest is very tight. All of this
is physical tension. She is pulling away from the force of gravity. Gravity, by
definition, allows the body to relax, and that calmness improves the ability
to respond. When you are tense somewhere in your body, you are, quite
literally, "holding on" to whatever it is that is causing you stress. In Erin's
case, she is worried about the test results, the cost of possible procedures,
and her son's increased pain. But Erin's worry is made all the worse by the
mounting physical tension in her own body.

Chances are that in the past you haven't paid a whole lot of attention to
being grounded, but now you need to cultivate your awareness of it so that
you learn to re-ground and stay calm. Observe how you become ungrounded as you interact with your children, spend your precious time on their
behalf, or silently worry about them, and use your journal to keep a record
of your observations. Particularly observe yourself during a tense discussion or argument because that is an environment that especially unseats us.

To help you identify the areas in your body where you habitually hold tension, look at the Tension Map that follows. Then ask yourself, *Where do I usually feel tension when I perform parental responsibilities?* Anywhere you are holding tension—anywhere that you are disconnecting—can be transformed and become a place of connection and calm relaxation instead—but only if you're aware of it first.

In which areas of your body do you usually hold tension?

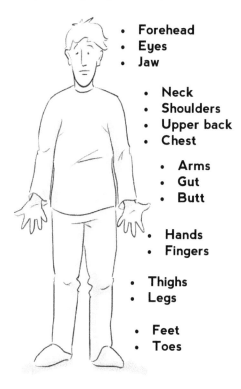

- **Forehead**
- **Eyes**
- **Jaw**

- **Neck**
- **Shoulders**
- **Upper back**
- **Chest**

- **Arms**
- **Gut**
- **Butt**

- **Hands**
- **Fingers**

- **Thighs**
- **Legs**

- **Feet**
- **Toes**

It is often useful to observe other people too. The next time you are on the bus, in the market, or standing in line at the bank just look around. We do not live in a relaxed society. You will see people with their shoulders hunched, or holding one of their hands in a tight fist, or making deep worried furrows in their forehead, marking the obvious places on the Tension Map. You can almost tell what they're feeling; all you have to do is remember what you felt like when you were tense in the same areas of your body.

In addition to the usual areas of tension (upper back, neck, jaw), there are also not-so-obvious places—in the toes, the tongue, behind the eyes, in the arches of the feet, to name a few. As you become more familiar with the obvious places where you store tension, you will start becoming aware of the deeper, subtler places. Once you are able to observe your entire body, you can use the tools for calming down to establish a more peaceful atmosphere for your family and you.

In the awareness section and with the use of the tension map of this chapter you identified the areas in your body where you hold tension. Now, let's use the tool of grounding to release that tension. Another name for grounding is letting go. This means just what it says. Let go of—release—wherever you are holding tension. Let gravity work. Let the tension flow out of you and into the ground. Practice this by tightly clenching an object in your hand. Start with something soft like a small stuffed animal, an old tennis ball, or a bunched up T-shirt. Now clench it really tightly and heighten that tension. Squeeze it even more tightly. Good. Now let go. Relax your hand muscles. The object will drop to the ground. Feel the wave of calm pass through your whole body.

To practice letting go in your body, try an exercise called the "Tension/Release Scan." This exercise is most efficient if performed in a place and a time that allows you peace and quiet.

EXERCISE:
TENSION/RELEASE SCAN

Sit comfortably in a chair, arms and legs uncrossed.
Tighten the muscles in your left foot and leg.
Now, with an exhale, release the leg muscles.
Tighten the muscles in your right foot and leg.
With an out-breath, release them.
Tighten the muscles in your belly.

Breathe out and release.
Tighten the muscles in your left hand and arm.
Breathe out and release.
Tighten the muscles in your right hand and arm.
Breathe out and release.
Tighten your chest and shoulders.
Breathe out and release.
Tighten your neck muscles.
Breathe out and release.
Tighten your jaw muscles.
Breathe out and release.
Tighten your whole face.
Breathe out and release.
Tighten your whole body.
Breathe out and release.

After this exercise, locate the area in your body where you store the most tension. Is it your jaw? Your lower back? Your legs? Wherever it is, feel the tension there, hold it, and even heighten it for five seconds. Now, on an out breath, let it go. Release the tension into the ground. At the same time feel yourself supported by the floor and chair (the first form of grounding). As you release tension in these muscles it is helpful to think about the situations that trigger you to tense up. Does it happen when your kid starts yelling, when your spouse doesn't mow the lawn, or when you don't know why your child is crying? Then, literally, let the tension in your muscles go. Let gravity draw them out. Doing this regularly sets you well on the way to calming down.

TOOL #3: SENSING

The third tool for calming yourself is sensing.

When we shut down one or more of our five senses we begin to disconnect.

Martin was working on a large electrical bid due the next morning. His wife was gone, and he was solely in charge of their four kids. Two were banging on pots and pans, one was playing video games, and one was rummaging through cupboards for food. As the pandemonium around him began to swell, Martin grew more and more stressed. This was a big bid, and it looked like he would be up all night. As his heart rate increased due to his quicker breathing and his headache worsened, he hunched forward and began to lose any sense of grounding. "I lost it," he said. "I wasn't able to focus on my bid or my kids. I became totally unproductive."

We can hear from Martin's own words ("I lost it") that he disconnected in the first two ways described in this chapter. He had abnormal breathing and was caught up in physical tension. But there was one more thing he said that was a clue, "I wasn't able to focus on my bid or my kids. I became totally unproductive."

Martin shut down his senses. He didn't hear or see the needs of his children, and he literally couldn't see what needed to be done on his bid. To get himself back on track, Martin took a deep calming breath, grounded himself, and began to use his senses. He heard the banging pans and saw the mess, and it helped him to become aware of the needs around him. He could now clearly see and hear what needed to be done and went to work. After he addressed the needs of his children, he was again able to focus on his bid.

The five senses are the gateways to our awareness. We see, smell, hear, taste, and touch the world. When we shut down in one or more of our five senses, as Martin did, we disconnect physically to what is around us. When we say, "He's out of touch," we usually deduce that the person is disconnected from reality. This means that the person who is out of touch is not in contact, through his senses, with what is going on around him right now. If he is not in touch with the present through his senses, he is literally disconnected from the world. Performance is all about how you manipulate and interact with the world right now, so you can see how disconnecting in the senses puts you at a disadvantage.

I noticed this when I was eating lunch the other day. All I was thinking about was an upcoming meeting at 3:00 pm. I was not tasting the food that was passing my lips. I forked the bite of potato salad into my mouth and swallowed it, but the physical, connected act of sensing the flavors, textures, and temperature of the food was absent. When I finally shifted my awareness, I put my attention on the sensory experiences of taste, smell, and sight. My stress instantly decreased several notches, because I was connected again to the present, not fretting about the impending event. Finally, I enjoyed the meal even though I still had the difficult meeting a little later. The meeting would either go well or not. "Right now," I thought, "I'm eating."

This is a very common experience for parents—preparing a meal and watching everyone inhale it without even chewing. Or, trying so hard to get the kids to stay at the table, or eat their broccoli, that they are not even aware of their senses. The meal becomes stressful and un-enjoyable. They are already thinking about the load of dishes to be done or the practice they will be late for. As they again become aware of their senses, the smells of the food, the texture, and the taste, it brings them to the present, and mealtime becomes more enjoyable.

The expression "Come to your senses!" has real import here. When you open up your senses you are connecting to what is going on right here, right now. This is important because performing as a parent always takes place in the now.

The other two ways of disconnecting (breathing and grounding) are fairly straightforward as far as parenting is concerned. But being connected through the senses is a little tricky, because being too open can also distract you. You don't necessarily want to let your attention focus on hearing your son's blaring music while you're trying to discuss a concern about dating with your teenage daughter, or focus on your sense of sight, seeing the dishes in the sink, when your sick child needs your love. The object of your senses is not an asset if it is upsetting, disturbing, or frustrating. You want to use your senses selectively so that you help, instead of hinder, your performance. In the next section I'll show you how to do that. Right now, all you have to do is become more aware of when you are shutting down in your senses. Use your journal to bring your attention to all five.

It is easy to turn on one of your five senses—seeing, hearing, touching, tasting, or smelling—when you become aware that you are anxious. As you make the connection through your senses to the world around you, you will start feeling calmer in your body.

What is the relationship between opening your senses and calming down?

Your senses connect you to the world. They tell you what you are looking at, listening to, tasting, touching, or smelling. Without your senses you wouldn't know where you were or what was happening around you. You would feel very disconnected, which would be frightening. A well-known psychology experiment proved this. When people were placed in a pitch-black, soundproof room they immediately became disoriented. Soon they grew severely anxious. Why? They had no reference points to anything familiar. They were cut-off and adrift, disconnected from any sensory input. Sensory input is connection, how we make contact with our world. Since stress is a function of disconnection, it makes logical and practical sense that to reduce stress, anxiety, and tension, you want to increase your connection, this time, through your senses.

Let's start with your sense of sight. Optometrists notice that when we are anxious, our sight tends to be compromised, as is reflected in the phrase, "He has tunnel vision." Commonly, we use the phrase to describe a person who is not taking in the whole picture. We might say, "John, who believes that charter schools and private schools are a waste of money, has tunnel vision when it comes to education for his children because he is unable or unwilling to see the other side's position." We conclude, "John is cut off."

Contrast this to a person who has a broader perspective, "Jane sees the necessity for parents to have options when it comes to giving their children what they think is best, while recognizing that overall most schools have great teachers and staff that do their best with what they have. She has a wider view." Jane may well have a position she feels passionately about, but her view of the overall situation is larger than the perspective of someone who can only see one side.

The narrow or expanded view isn't just an attitudinal state; it's a real visual connection through the sense of sight. When you open up your sense of sight you can actually reduce stress in your system. This is true for the other senses as well. When you do so you will feel calmer.

Let's work on your sense of sight by starting with the following simple exercise. It is meant to open up your sense of sight by expanding your peripheral vision.

EXERCISE: TAPPING INTO THE BIG PICTURE

Sit comfortably and look straight ahead of you.

Keeping your head still, move both of your eyes all the way to the left, and see how much you can see.

Bring your eyes back to center. Breathe.

Now move your eyes all the way to the right. See as much as you can see to the right.

Bring them back to center. Breathe.

Now look up as high as you can. See as much as you can above you.

Now bring your eyes back to center. Breathe.

And now look down, all the way down.

And back to center.

Breathe.

Now, look straight ahead of you.

You have just expanded your vision in four directions. Notice how much more you can see now than you were aware of before you started this exercise.

Breathe, ground, and feel the calm throughout your body.

Why would expanding your vision be a calming experience? The short answer is that when you are able to relax your eyes, you calm your whole body down because you have opened your peripheral vision and tapped into your parasympathetic nervous system. It all has to do with how the human nervous system works.

Your nervous system has two branches, the sympathetic and the parasympathetic, and each branch serves a different and complementary function. The sympathetic nervous system regulates arousal; it amps you up and keeps you alert. The parasympathetic system regulates relaxation; it calms you down. When a perceived danger is lurking, your sympathetic nervous system kicks in, sounding an alarm and sending warning signals to the brain. Danger! Watch out! Adrenaline flows. Blood starts pumping. Your gut tightens. Your breath shortens. The "fight or flight" response takes over, and you either attack the oncoming threat, or you run away from it. In contrast, when the danger is passed, your body needs to settle, to be quiet, to rest. That's when the parasympathetic system takes over. We need both systems because they balance one another. If we were on alert all the time (sympathetic) we'd be freaked out, and if we were relaxed all the time (parasympathetic) we'd be flaked out.

How does all of this relate to your eyes and to calming down?

Our sense of vision has two parts, the central vision and the peripheral vision, and each part is hardwired to a different branch of your nervous system. You use your central vision, which is connected to your sympathetic nervous system, to identify what is coming toward you or what is right in front of you. Whether you are staring at a ferocious mountain lion or reading a road sign, when your central vision is turned on, your system is at least somewhat aroused. On the other hand, when you are taking in "the big picture" and your peripheral vision, which is wired to your parasympathetic nervous system, is turned on, you are calming down.

Have you ever been cleaning the house and found yourself so focused on the mess everyone made but left you to clean up alone— that you fail to notice anything else? You don't hear the baby crying, the TV playing, or the phone ringing. You don't see that your son needs help with his homework or that dinner is burning. You are using only your central vision. You are placing a high demand on your sympathetic nervous system, putting you in a continuous state of arousal. The more you focus on the objects in front of you, the more you amp yourself up without even realizing it, causing yourself to become flustered, overwhelmed, and tense. You may try to convince yourself having to clean up alone is what is causing your anxiety and agitated reaction. But actually the problem is the strain you are putting on your sympathetic nervous system. No wonder you feel wired by the time you go to bed. Now would be a good time to let your parasympathetic nervous system take over, balance you out, and calm you down. Stop focusing on your teenager's dirty socks strewn across the floor and their overly expensive shoes, and look around. Shift from using your central vision to your peripheral vision. Use your eyes to scan the entire area, taking in everything around you. See your teenager playing video games on the couch. Look at your family picture on the wall, and the snow falling outside. See that there is more to your life than the candy wrappers on the floor in front of you.

What we have just done with your eyes, you also can do with one or another of your senses, though a bit differently with each one. Are you "stress-eating" because your child has graduated high school and is moving out? Are you mindlessly putting your hand in a bag of potato chips, putting chip after chip in your mouth, and never tasting their salty crispness? Try smelling it, tasting it, and feeling its texture on your tongue.

Did you suddenly enjoy your indulgent potato chip moment or did you realize it doesn't really taste good, and set it aside, using the tools to reduce your stress instead of simply stuffing food into your mouth? When you're packing the kids into the car, do you take a moment to notice the colors of the flowers or leaves on the trees? These seconds of sensory connection can go a long way to keeping your stress level at a more even keel.

Work on your sense of hearing by opening up to the sounds immediately around you (maybe those being made by your own body first). Then hear the sounds in the room, then the sounds just outside of the room, and then the sounds outside of the building and beyond.

Work on your sense of touch by feeling the different textures of your clothes next to your body or the carpet on your toes. How does your shirt or blouse feel next to your arms and chest? What does the fabric of your pants feel like next to your legs? If you're holding a sleeping baby feel his weight and firmness in your arms. Feel the softness of his skin and the fluffy blanket around him. (As you are doing this, continue to breathe and ground yourself.)

Connecting with your senses is an effective way of staying in the present and reducing tension and anxiety. Your senses are always available and are the best tools you have to connect you to the here and now. It is remarkable to me how unaware people are of what is right around them, and how infrequently they actually use their senses to help themselves feel calm.

This tool—sensing—can help you particularly when you are in the throes of stress. Sandra shared an experience she had while walking with her daughter:

> I was on auto pilot as I was walking with my daughter to school. She had not been feeling well for some time. We had taken her to the pediatrician and the chiropractor. We had changed her diet and tried essential oils. We had asked her if there was anything stressful going on at school or with friends. Nothing was working. Every morning was a fight because she didn't feel well and didn't

want to go to school. But she had already missed so much. I was so consumed in my thoughts about my daughter; I could feel my grip tighten on the stroller I was pushing.

We were walking up a large hill at the time. When we reached the top I turned around to see a panoramic picture of the valley. Its beauty surprised me, and I immediately calmed down, took some much-needed deep breaths, and enjoyed what was around me. Suddenly, I could feel the breeze on my face and smell the earth around me. By opening my senses, my entire outlook changed, and I had the calming sense that everything would be okay.

Often parents start fretting about what's going to happen and imagine the worst; all kinds of other negative scenarios shoot us into the future or yank us back to the past and work us up. If you're worked up, then *calm down*. Connect through your senses. Right here, right now. Breathe. Be grounded. Do it. It works.

PERSONAL INVENTORY: TAKING STOCK

If you own a business, and you want it to run successfully, you have to take stock periodically. That means stepping back, assessing the situation, and asking questions: What's going well and what needs improvement? Where's the surplus and where's the deficit? Since, for our purposes, you are in the business of being a parent, and we want you to run successfully, let's pause and take a personal inventory of your parenting habits around being calm.

Before writing this book I conducted a workshop for parents, and I asked them about their productive and unproductive actions around being calm. The unproductive parents were a mess: worrying, tensing up, holding everything inside, yelling too much, not getting enough sleep, eating too much junk food, drinking caffeinated beverages, having irregular meal-times, not exercising enough, taking meds just to survive, spending too much time online, watching TV or gaming, working too much, and staying angry. Remember, being calm has to do with what you're doing with your body, so all of the actions just mentioned involve or have a negative effect on the body.

On the other hand, the productive parents identified actions they take which have a positive effect on the body: getting enough sleep, taking a walk around the block, eating healthy food, having regular mealtimes, exercising, taking breaks, meditation, creating a schedule, praying, listening to calming music, reading spiritual texts, going for a bike ride, spending time with their partner or children, and visualizing calm places in nature.

I want you to take time to reflect on your actions and habits that support being calm, particularly if you feel "stressed out" a lot of the time. Start by answering these questions in a journal:

- What are you doing physically that is contributing to your feeling stressed out?
- What are you doing to keep yourself calm?

By keeping an inventory you are taking stock. You're stepping back and looking at what can make your performance—"the business of parenting," if you will—more successful.

The three core tools for being calm are breathing, grounding, and sensing, and as you use these tools over and over, you will be cultivating the productive habits of being calm.

Right now your main task is to cultivate your awareness and use the tools:

- When are you not calm?
- What's going on in your body then?
- Which tool or tools do you use to calm down?
  - Breathing?
  - Grounding?
  - Sensing?

QUICK CHECK-IN: CALM

When you are anticipating a stressful situation or challenge or are currently in one, stop and . . .

- Become aware of and acquainted with your unproductive habits. Notice when you are not calm (jittery, thoughts racing, anxiety).
    - Are you tense in some part of your body? (shoulders? stomach? jaw?)
    - Are you having anxious thoughts?
    - Are you holding your breath?
- Use the tools to cultivate productive habits.
- Breathe deeply down to your belly and lower back three times. Breathe in through your nose and out through your mouth.
- Ground yourself (feet on the floor, butt and back in the chair).
- Open your senses (see the colors, feel the fabrics, hear the sounds).
- Stay in this state for a few minutes.
- Return to whatever you were doing, staying calm and connected in your body.

One mother confronted me after an attempt to use the calming tools. She was quite ticked off. "I've done the breathing thing," she said, meaning, "That didn't work. Now what?"

There is no other now or what. Breathing is a lifelong activity. It takes time to become practiced at being more aware of your breath. It takes time to increase body awareness and to consciously use the tools to stay calm and present. You are reversing old habits of a lifetime, so be patient with yourself. If you have trouble remembering to prompt your awareness, I encourage you to use my CD, "Dr. B's Gentle Prompts for Calming Down." On it you will hear my voice prompting you at varying intervals to breathe and ground and sense. The more you hear these reminders, the more your system is being trained to remind yourself.

Here is an example from my co-author Michelle on how she is working to make the calming tools part of her every day routine:

Sometimes it's hard for me to become aware or remember what to do when the stress of parenting or life strikes. I wondered how I could improve before I ever reached my maximum patience allowance for my children and the stress they inevitably initiate. I began to practice the calming principles every day after picking my kids up from school. The bus drops them off by the park, so we all take some time to enjoy the outdoors before heading home.

No matter how stressed I am or what the stress is about, this ritual unwinds me. I always start by closing my eyes and taking a few deep breaths. I take off my shoes and feel the grass between my toes, feeling the power and draw of the earth. As I open my eyes I take a panoramic picture of everything around me. I see the cars on the freeway, the massive mountains, the trees, houses, and changing colors of the season.

This is usually the point when I become aware that my brow is furrowed, and I remember to relax and enjoy. This is the moment when I let my cares and worries blow away or sink into the earth. I watch the kids playing and hear their laughter waft through the rustling of the trees and the buzz of car engines. I smell fall in the air as the wind blows and tickles my face. No matter what is bothering me, I begin to appreciate all of the wonderful things around me and find myself more grateful then when I came. My perspective of life changes, because I have moved out of the box I work in all day and now can enjoy something much larger and grander.

I'm hoping this little ritual will help the three calming tools become second nature to me. So that when the stresses of parenting strike, I am prepared to be successful in managing the challenges thrown my way.

Consistency is the key: decide that you are going to use the calming tools regularly. Check in with yourself often, especially during stress-producing situations. Ask yourself, *What is my body doing right now?* This awareness will become more and more refined as you commit yourself to calming down. And as soon as you are aware of how you are disconnecting in your body, use one or more of the three tools: breathing, grounding, and sensing. That's all there are: three. And they're available to you at every waking moment.

QUESTION & ANSWER

Michelle: As parents it sometimes feels like too much to use all of these calming tools at once. Do you have any advice for us on how to get started? If we remember nothing else what is the one thing we definitely must do?

Dr. B: Breathing! Recently, I had a parent tell me, "I don't have time to breathe." I paused and looked at him compassionately. "No time to breathe?" I think what he meant was, "I don't have time to pay attention to my breath and to use the calming tools." My response? "You're breathing all the time anyway. You might as well learn to consciously use your breath to help you win when it comes to parenting. It will take a few seconds, but it will also make a big difference in how you perform overall."

Another very effective exercise, which pulls together all of the tools in this chapter, is called "The Wedge." It's like pressing the restart button and will give you a new spurt of attention and energy. It takes only a few seconds to learn, and even less to use once you are practiced at it.

 ## EXERCISE:
THE WEDGE

As you exhale, close your eyes and let them rest.
Feel the breath go down the front of your body and into the
floor.
Now breathe in, feeling the breath coming up the back of your
body and up to the top of your head.

When it reaches the top of your head, open your eyes.

The Wedge is great because it combines all three calming tools—breathing, grounding, and sensing. Parents who use the wedge are more successful in parenting than those who let stress in their body mount and overwhelm them.

CHAPTER 6

How to Be Confident

TIED UP IN "NOTS"?

Three different parents, Devon, Joy, and Patrick, shared some of their frustrations with parenting. Devon talked about his presentation at work. "I got up in front of the room, and all I could think was that I was up all night with my crying son. I'm not as prepared as I should be. How can I compete with these guys who have no kids? They're going to think I'm so unprofessional. It's going to be hard for me to keep my mind on what I am speaking about." Joy, in the high school principal's office, trying to help her daughter with a scheduling issue, thought, "I don't know how to do this without being too intense; I'm going to scare the principal away. Whenever I get upset I always ramble and say stupid things. I'm not good at staying calm in confrontational situations." As she told me this she sighed, "In fact, I was so over the top that I embarrassed my daughter, and she asked me not to take care of things at school anymore." Patrick, working to help his son with a math problem, started thinking, "I can't get this, and I can't keep my cool. I'm going to explode!" and he did.

Devon, Joy, and Patrick were all describing one of the toughest experiences a parent could have: losing self-confidence when he or she has to do something challenging. At the moment when you have to perform and your mind starts broadcasting negative thoughts—*I'm not prepared; I don't know how to be patient; I can't stay calm*—you're all tied up in negativity—in "nots": *I'm not kind enough. I'm not an organized person. I'm not a good listener. I'm not a good mom.* Of course, all this negativity makes you feel horrible about yourself. The anxiety and self-doubt quickly turn into a self-fulfilling prophecy. Suddenly, you don't know what to say in an argument, you discipline too harshly, and you lash out at your mother in-law when she tells you that you aren't spending enough time with your children. With all this negativity, your stress level soars, and your performance suffers, no matter what you're doing and no matter how much you want to be a good parent.

If you want to be successful in your parenting, you need self-confidence—positive feelings about yourself. You have to believe that you can be a successful parent, you do have time, and your best is good enough. It's the same self-fulfilling prophecy I mentioned just above, but this time in a positive direction. When you believe in yourself you are much more likely to perform well.

Many people feel confident at work, with friends, and doing hobbies, but as parents their confidence fades in and out as stress mounts. In this chapter we'll discuss where confidence comes from, how to find it in yourself, and how to retrieve it quickly when you feel it slipping away.

CONFIDENCE: IT'S ALL IN YOUR MIND

How does confidence fit into our model of the three-legged stool? One of the legs stands for your mind. Your self-confidence is determined in large part by what is going on in your mind. Remember our personal chatter-box, our talk-radio station that we discussed earlier? It is this station that broadcasts a steady stream of thoughts that compare, encourage, criticize, evaluate, and judge everything inside and outside of you.

When it comes to your performance as a parent, your mind broadcasts an ongoing, often contradictory monologue about yourself: *I'm terrible at communication. I'm good at playing with the little kids. I'll never be able to keep my house clean. I always do well at getting to the kid's activities. I'm not making enough money. I'm not good at communicating with my children . . .* and on it goes.

When your mind produces positive, affirming, encouraging thoughts like: *I can do this, I've got what it takes, I am making it through,* you feel confident. You have faith in yourself. You believe you will succeed and you move ahead with assurance. But if your mind is broadcasting negative self-statements: *I'm not a good housekeeper, I'll never be a fun dad, I don't know what to say to my kids,* then you are swamped in self-doubt. You don't trust yourself. This is utterly distracting, and the deficit of confidence can seriously hurt your ability to perform well.

As we continue, we will discuss what it takes to make your mind work for you. To do this we will examine what confidence actually is and look at how your mind affects your parenting performance positively and negatively.

WHAT IS CONFIDENCE?

The word confidence is made up of two Latin roots: *con,* meaning "with," and *fidelis,* which means "faith" or "trust." A confident person has faith in herself and trusts that she can accomplish the task.

Fidelis has an additional meaning, and that is loyalty. We can interpret this to mean that a confident person is also loyal to herself. When she's facing a difficult situation she doesn't jump ship. She believes she can deal with it and stays with the process right to the end.

If you struggle with self-confidence—and most parents do at one time or another—when the going gets rough—like when your daughter is diagnosed with a serious disability, or your son is failing at school—you may feel like you want to bolt. Not because you don't love your child, but because you want the best for her and you don't know how to give it to her. You may find yourself saying, *I can't handle this. I wish things could be easier.*

Though these feelings are understandable, wanting to bolt creates a problem because it means your attention isn't fully present. It's on its way out the door. In every situation you face as a parent, you need your mind to stand by you, to support and encourage you through thick and thin, not turn against you and undermine the process. When your mind is yelling, *Let me out of here!* it is a way of abandoning yourself, which we can certainly call a form of disloyalty. And besides, how realistic is it for you to think about jumping ship as a parent? You can't and you won't.

When both of Maggie's young children were crying at once, she thought, *I can't take this anymore! I've tried everything! I'm done!* When Bart worked day in and day out, wearing himself out to provide for his boys, and never received a single thank you, his thoughts were similar. *Why do I even bother? I have done everything I can for them, but it's never enough. I give up!* Your children and your partner (if you have one) depend on your being there for them. You have to train your mind to be loyal, to have faith in your ability, and to trust that you can do the job of parenting as well as you can. For Maggie, being loyal to herself would sound more like, *This is hard, but I've done it before, and I can do it again.* For Bart it may be, *I work because I love my kids. I know I can keep it up and have a positive attitude.*

STAYING GROUNDED IN YOURSELF AND LOYAL TO YOURSELF

When you glance around at other parents it may look to you like they are fully engaged. They can do it. They know all the tricks, they're not tired, and they don't look overwhelmed. What's the matter with me? I can tell you, after working with thousands of parents over many years, you are projecting onto them a sense of certainty and security they probably don't have. Most other parents, from time to time, are also fiercely battling negative self-talk. They feel overpowered by life. They may appear calm and focused, just as you might look like that to them, but at times inside they also want to wave their white flag, surrender, and retreat.

It is important you stay grounded in yourself and loyal to yourself. We spend entirely too much time looking at and comparing ourselves with other people. It is an unproductive habit, and we would do well to nip it. If you want to improve in your own parenting, evaluate what it is *you* need to do to improve. While you may learn something from watching others, ultimately, you will have to do it in your own way, whatever "it" is—whether it's disciplining your toddler, preparing a family dinner, or supporting your children in their extracurricular activities. Keep your focus on yourself and what you need to do to improve.

NEGATIVITY AND DISCONNECTION

We discussed earlier that your self-evaluating, talk-radio mind has two sides: positive and negative. When you focus on negativity you are disconnecting from the positive side of your mind, the one that wants to support you on your path to be the best parent you can. When Jason's mind got stuck on the thought, *I'm not a good dad*, he couldn't see all the great things he'd done with and for his kids.

Remember our basic formula: stress is a function of disconnection. The more negative things you say about yourself (the more you disconnect from the positive side of your mind), the more your stress will build. This will cause you to question your judgment, and you'll become increasingly prone to errors. The self-fulfilling prophecy will take over. Clearly, your performance will be compromised.

AWARENESS FIRST

In the last chapter we applied the two-step strategy below to disconnection in your body in order to remain calm.

Step 1: Become aware of the signs that your stress is building because you are disconnecting, and

Step 2: Use specific tools to reconnect yourself, lower your stress level, and boost your performance.

In this section we are going to apply the same two-step process to your mind to give you confidence. Let's start with your awareness of what is going on there and examine your negative thoughts about yourself and your parenting.

THE CATALOG OF NEGATIVITY

There are several ways your mind broadcasts negativity about yourself, and they all are disconnections from your positive self. They all undermine self-confidence. As you read the descriptions below, see which ones characterize your self-talk when you are facing a parenting situation:

1. **You doubt yourself.** Your internal monologue is riddled with sentences that begin with the words: *I can't . . . I don't . . . and I'm not.* For example, *I can't parent with love and logic; even my own father says I don't have the patience for it. I'm not focused enough.* You doubt your abilities and are caught up in a downward spiral.

2. **You believe there is something wrong with you or that you are a bad person.** These thoughts sound like you're a mess. *I can never do enough. I'm not positive. I don't remember anything. I'm not compassionate. I'm so mean.* You believe that the very fact that you are having these thoughts proves that you are deficient and probably not fixable.

3. **You regret the past.** You are brooding over what you should have done and didn't. *I shouldn't have let her hang out with those boys. They had a terrible influence on her. Now I've ruined her life and mine. I'll*

never make up for that. You berate yourself about the opportunities you missed or caused your children to miss, or blame yourself for the choices they made.

4. **You imagine the worst (projecting into the future). Your negativity extends into the indeterminate future.** *I know exactly what's going to happen when my kids go to college. They are going to blow all their money if they even earn any and then expect me to pay for their school. Then they'll waste away my money in stupid video games, flunk out, and move back home. I'm not even going to bother saving the money or helping them fill out applications. It's a waste of my time.* You feel like you might as well give up.

5. **You feel helpless and alone.** You feel that nothing you can do will change the situation and that no one will help you. *I just don't have a chance. There is too much peer pressure on my kids to get involved in destructive things. I can't be home with them after school. I just don't have the time. I have to work. All I have is me, and that's not much.* You feel lonely and perhaps desperate. This is particularly true for single parents.

6. **You fear humiliation and retribution.** You imagine a negative reaction from a neighbor, child's teacher, or friend if you perform your parenting responsibilities poorly. You believe they are saying (or whispering): *You should watch your kids more closely. I would never let my daughter wear those clothes. You are a terrible housekeeper. You are so mean to your children! Your child shouldn't be missing so much school! Do you really consider yourself a responsible parent?* This only makes your negative feelings about yourself worse.

7. **You worry that history will repeat itself.** If you have had trouble raising one of your children, you are probably thinking, *I messed up her brother royally, so there's no way I can do any better this time. I don't even know where I went wrong. There's no hope for the younger ones. My Mom couldn't get the parenting thing right, and neither can I.*

8. **Your thinking becomes disorganized.** While you are in a challenging situation—like confronting another parent about their child's inappropriate treatment of your child—you find that what you say doesn't conform to the way you ordered the material in your mind. All sense of organization becomes unglued and loses any consistent pattern it may have had. Your mind feels like a chaotic mess. *I forgot what I was going to say. I don't remember exactly what happened. I can't think! I don't remember anything! My memory is as full of holes as a pound of Swiss cheese!*

9. **You become superstitious.** You start thinking that the everyday little things in life—the way you did your daughters hair, the coffee cup you choose, the way you drive to work—have a direct impact on your parenting performance. *The last time I put a bow in my daughter's hair, she got so nervous about getting up in front of her class. Definitely no more bows!* While this kind of thinking might not seem negative to you, it does indicate that you feel powerless over your performance and that other things are controlling it.

10. **Other possibilities.** Perhaps there is some other way that negativity shows up in your mind. If so, write it down in your journal.

YOUR OWN CATALOG

How you use your mind to talk to yourself makes all the difference.

My co-author, Michelle, recently shared some events with me that occurred in her life as a parent. These events had her questioning her own self-confidence and abilities as a parent. See if you can pick out a few of the negative self-statements going on in her chatterbox and how they affected her confidence, stress, and ability to perform optimally.

"What's wrong with me?" "Have I done something wrong?" "Am I not being a good parent?" Usually I'm pretty confident in my parenting capabilities but I have been questioning myself and my luck today as I bring my oldest daughter Ella, who's ten, home from the hospital. About a week and a half ago she was slammed in the face by another kid's knee in gym class. Poor thing, it broke her nose, and today she had to have it straightened. Things like this happen all the time, but my concern is that our family has been inundated with injury as of late. Let me give you the history of the last month and a half.

About two months before Ella broke her nose, my five-year-old, Julia, was swinging on her bunk bed like a little chimp. Her brother Jackson, age two, thought she needed a little more momentum and liveliness in her swinging and proceeded to give her a hefty push. He's stronger than most two-year-olds, and Julia went sailing, landing on her arm . . . it broke.

Just before Julia got her neon yellow cast off, Jackson was out with Grandma and Grandpa for an ice cream treat. As he ran out of the ice cream shop, the door closed before his little hands were clear of the door—crunch. Stupid door! I thought it was probably broken, but I figured there isn't much they can do for a pinky, and I knew he would never keep a splint on. Two weeks later when his finger was still swollen, I decided to take him to the pediatrician just to make sure. When the doctor called me in with a, "Why don't you come and take a look at these x-rays," I knew it was bad. It was very bad. The top of his pinkly bone was broken off, facing the wrong direction, and floating. The bottom of the pinky was cracked down the side. I immediately started berating myself. "I am the worst mom ever! How could I have waited so long!" Feeling miserable inside, I took the pediatricians referral to the orthopedic hand specialist and darted out of the office.

At least I was right about one thing—Jackson would not keep his splint on. I was constantly chasing him around the house picking up the tape and the brace and reapplying. The specialist finally put a cast on his finger and assured me there was hope that he wouldn't have to have a pin surgically put in if we could keep the finger immobilized.

I am constantly filled with worry that something will happen to one of the kids that will make things worse, and what if I don't take care of the wounds correctly? What about my eight-year-old, Daniel? Nothing has happened to him yet. I'm just waiting. I am so stressed about keeping the kids safe. I follow them around so much it's hard to focus on the other things in my life that need attention—the laundry, house, work, my husband—and, of course, I feel guilty because I forgot to call my in-laws and let them know what was going on. I am definitely not being successful, and I'm embarrassed that my kids have had so many injuries. I know I can't control it, but people still make comments.

Had Michelle turned her talk radio dial to more positive self-statements, she realizes she would have had a much easier, more positive, and less stressful experience with her children and herself.

WHAT'S GOING ON IN YOUR CHATTERBOX?

As you continue on with this next exercise—designed to develop your awareness of the "less-than" messages your mind produces—think of your own stressful circumstances.

EXERCISE: YOUR INNER CHORUS (NEGATIVE)

Sit with your feet on the floor and breathe deeply down to your belly.

After you feel quiet, fill in the chart below by following this procedure:

1. For each category below read the question on the right.
2. Close your eyes.
3. See the answer on your "inner screen."
4. Open your eyes.
5. Record your answers in your journal.

Negative Thinking	What are your negative, self-doubting thoughts about yourself and your parenting? What do you say to yourself that starts with: "I can't." "I don't." or "I'm not."?
Regretting the Past	What are three regrets you have about how you performed as a parent in the past?
Imagining the Worst	State three things you are afraid will happen if your parenting is below par.
Feeling Hopeless and Helpless	What do you feel hopeless or helpless about in regard to your abilities and performance as a parent? List three things.
Fearing Humiliation and Retribution	Who will be disappointed or angry if you parent poorly? What will they say or do? Name three people.
Worrying that History will Repeat Itself	What unrewarding experiences have you had with parenting in the past that you worry you'll have again?
Disorganized Thinking	Describe what happens to your thinking when your mind is clouded with negative, self-doubting thoughts about your parenting?
Other Forms of Negativity	Are there any other ways your mind broadcasts negativity about how you are as a parent? If so, write them down.

THE LITANY LOOP

Gary, who had always been a successful businessman and happy father of two boys, became overly discouraged when he lost his job. He applied and interviewed for numerous positions but was turned away from each one with the usual, "You're over qualified . . . We're currently not hiring . . . Try again in six months." Though Gary had heard all of this several times he continued to take the news badly, thinking, *I'm just not good enough. I don't have the skills. I can't take care of my boys like I want to.*

I can't . . . I don't . . . I'm not . . . Gary's mind was a catalog of painful self–put downs, setting him up for a year of feeling badly about himself and failing to get a job. This thinking—the same three sentences—played out over and over again for Gary in almost any situation in his life, especially in his interactions with his children. He was trapped in a cycle of unfavorable thinking that began and ended with negative thoughts about himself.

I call this a "litany loop." It's a personal list of fearful outcomes that you repeat over and over again from which there is no escape, and which leads you to fulfill the negative predictions. You tell yourself you aren't good enough to succeed and—surprise—you don't succeed. You believe you can't perform—and you can't perform. You think you don't have a chance—and you don't seize the chances that come your way. This loop has a quasi-religious flavor (the "litany" part) because you keep repeating it over and over again, as if you are devoted to it. How can you possibly do well when your mind, one of the three key players on your team, is down-right devoted to being negative about you and your chances?

If your self-confidence is low, the first step in reversing the process is to become aware of your personal litany loop of negativity. If it's going on behind a curtain, you can't possibly fight it. I have found that every parent has his or her own list of negative self-statements; a personal repertoire of I can'ts, I don'ts, and I'm nots, that start spinning whenever one faces a challenging parenting situation.

At this point, you have two options:

Option 1. You can keep repeating these sentences, mantra-like, and watch a self-fulfilling prophecy inexorably unfold ("He who believes he will fail, will fail."). This would be akin to going backwards, or at best, standing still and being stuck. Surprisingly, this is what most people default to, because it doesn't occur to them that there is an alternative.

Option 2. You can decide, right now, that you want to shift out of this gear-to-nowhere, and learn how to transform these thoughts, so your mind can help, not hinder, you.

I strongly encourage you to pick Option 2 and continue on the road to transformation. To venture out on this path, you must decide right now that negativity is not going to be your companion. Tell yourself clearly and strongly, "I don't want to be stuck in these self-defeating thoughts any longer. When one comes up, I will acknowledge it is there, but I won't play into it. I won't fan its fire by repeating it over and over inside my head. I'll remind myself that my less-than thoughts and bad feelings about myself and parenting are road signs telling me that I'm disconnecting. As soon as I become aware of them, I'll use the tools to reconnect and build my self-confidence."

STAY IN THE PRESENT

When you are disconnecting in your mind and thinking negatively, you are not only subtracting yourself, but you are also taking yourself out of the present moment.

Samantha was helping her daughter with her math homework. Math has never been a strong subject for her and when she saw the division problem she thought, *I don't remember how to do this. I haven't taken a math class for twenty years.* What time zone is Samantha in when she's thinking that? Is she in the present? No. Most likely she has one leg in the past, based on her previous disastrous experiences with her own math homework as a student. And Samantha could have one leg in the future, projecting forward into a time when her child fails math because she couldn't help her. But this present moment is neither the past nor the future. In this moment Samantha can either go down in flames, or, like the phoenix, she can rise from the ashes. She can slide into a pit of bad feelings and anxiety, or she can tell herself, *I have the chance to make things differ-ent—I can Google how to solve long division, I can call my sister-in-law who's a math teacher, or I can hire a math tutor. I can help my daughter right now.* Samantha can choose her direction.

The human mind is famous for flip-flopping from the past to the future and then back again. Reverse, fast-forward, reverse, fast-forward, reverse, fast-forward. Imagine doing that to your car over and over. You'll strip the gears and the car will be stuck in your driveway. You can't go anywhere. That's what your negative thinking is doing to your mind. It's immobilizing you.

The truth is that the past is gone. The future hasn't happened yet. The present is the moment of action. It is your field of possibility.

THE THREE TOOLS FOR BUILDING CONFIDENCE

We are going to work on the three key tools for gaining and strengthen-ing your confidence through a series of exercises. With guided imagery, I will ask you to close your eyes and then direct you through a sequence of pictures in your imagination. This is the technique of choice used in sport psychology. Athletes are performing every moment on the field, court, or in the pool. Their confidence is being tested all the time. If it starts to falter, they can't afford to stop the action to talk to their coach or call their coun-selor; they have to re-strengthen immediately. Guided imagery provides the tools. It's the same thing when you are parenting. If you run into a difficult situation and your confidence starts to slip, you need an "inner toolbox" to strengthen your confidence right away. Guided imagery will train you to do that.

TOOL #1: CONFIDE

EXERCISE: CONFIDE IN YOUR CONFIDANT

Sit in a comfortable position, preferably in a straight-backed chair. Uncross your arms and legs and close your eyes.

Breathe deeply down to your belly.

Feel your feet supported by the floor and your legs, butt, and back supported by the chair.

Choose one of the negative self-statements from your litany loop and start repeating it over to yourself (e.g. I'm not good enough!).

See in your mind's eye what you look like when you are thinking the self-defeating thought. How does that affect your posture? Your facial expression?

How do you feel: physically? emotionally? spiritually?

Once you have a clear image of how you look and feel, sweep all of that negativity out to the left.

Now imagine yourself looking into a mirror, but at the moment, the mirror is empty.

Now see who comes into the mirror. It's the image of your highest, best, most shining self. If that image doesn't come easily, then see someone you can confide in, someone who has confidence in you, someone you trust. It can be a spouse, partner, parent, sibling, relative, friend, or a colleague. It can be someone living or someone who has passed on. It can be a spiritual entity.

See the image of your highest self, or whoever has come into the mirror, very clearly. This is your confidant.

Tell it the negativity that is going on in your mind. Don't hold back anything.

Confide what you are thinking in sentences that start with: *I can't, I don't,* or *I'm not.* (I can't do this. I'm not good at this parenting thing. I don't have what it takes.)

See the confidant receiving everything you have to say without criticizing, evaluating, or judging you.

Open your eyes.

Let's explore what just happened.

First, who came into your mirror as your confidant? Here is a short list of those who often appear: your highest self, your spouse, your counselor, your pastor (priest, or rabbi), your dad or mom, Jesus, Allah, God, a grandparent, or guardian angel.

This person is your confidant, if only for this moment. The next time you use the exercise, the person or entity may change, but trust that this is the best confidant for you to confide in right now.

Sometimes people feel "weird" about who or what appears. Each of us has someone or something special to confide in. Don't judge the choice, just trust it.

Why is confiding the first tool in building confidence? Because when you are holding onto and hiding your bad feelings about yourself, you feel terrible. The feelings become very heavy, and, like quicksand, they suck you into despair. Not only are you disconnecting from anything positive inside of you, but also from people around you who might offer support.

Perhaps you're afraid that if you tell others what you really feel about yourself and your abilities, you'll look irresponsible and weak in their eyes. To avoid the humiliation of what you perceive to be a massive parenting failure, you pull away from others, including people who might support you. But the isolation only causes you to feel even worse about yourself, causing more stress at a critical time when true support from others who care about you and your children could be very helpful. We all need the encouragement that comes from those who are close to us. Without it, we agonize silently and feel lost.

Julie's son recently vandalized a piece of public property. "I can't really talk with anyone about it," Julie said. "I feel like everyone is judging me and looking down on me. I feel responsible for what happened, because he's my son. I thought I taught him better than that. I quit socializing altogether, and I stay by myself. I avoid talking to anyone."

Feeling stuck inside yourself is a sad place to be, but this is how many parents feel when they lose confidence in themselves. They feel isolated and immobilized. While it is true you may be a single mom or dad, or your neighbors haven't experienced the things you have as a parent, that doesn't mean you have no support. And you are not really stuck—you just feel stuck. When you confide these negative emotions, when you let them out, you move away from this disconnected, lonely place. You unload these feelings about yourself to someone who will not judge or criticize you, and, in turn, you find relief.

Once you've confided, you are ready for the second tool.

TOOL #2: REFLECT

EXERCISE:
RECEIVING THE POSITIVE REFLECTION

Let's continue with the imagery exercise.
Sit comfortably, with your back well supported.
Breathe deeply and ground yourself.
Close your eyes.
See your confidant in the mirror.
Your confidant, who has just heard your negative thoughts and feelings, now responds. It reflects back to you something

accurate and positive about yourself in response to what you confided. It speaks to you in sentences that start with: *you can, you do,* and *you are.* Listen to what it is saying to you and receive the positive reflection.

Thank the confidant for its support. (Remember "Thank You" from the last chapter?).

Breathe in and out.

Open your eyes.

Let's look at what happened. First, what did the image in the mirror reflect back to you? Contemplate it for a moment and write it in your journal.

Here are some of the things mirrors reflect back to my clients and parents:

"You are capable. Jump in!"

"You've handled difficult children before. You can do it again."

"You can figure out what to do."

"You have what it takes."

"You can make time."

"You can do well, because you've worked hard."

"You can do hard things."

"You are patient enough."

This tool—reflect—is necessary for two reasons.

First, when the mind is stuck in negative feelings, we completely forget about our genuinely positive and potentially helpful inner voice. Why are we always stuck listening to the discouraging voice? Mostly, it's a matter of habit. Though I believe we are all born with the potential to feel good about ourselves, there are, unfortunately, forces that negate and disempower us. In our culture and in our personal lives, they often hold more sway than those that help us build a strong inner confidence and competency.

Remember what I said earlier about the media? Turn on the television any time of day or night, and it is filled with messages that are basically negative—you need to drive a different car, use a different spaghetti sauce, buy these toys, pay for that tutoring—all telling you that you are not a good enough parent as you are. All too often, parents reinforce this negativity with their constant competition and comparison. Rather than nurture the positive messages, they inundate themselves with the message, "You are not good enough." If you keep dwelling on the negative, you are bound to feel terrible about yourself. Remember: negative in mathematics is less than zero.

You are not less than zero.

You need to have reflected back to yourself the positive things about yourself as a parent that you may have forgotten or that you don't pay attention to, either not enough or not at all. You need to hear positive, affirming things about yourself, so you can feel empowered.

One mother I worked with, Liz, was discouraged with her ability to make choices saying, "My kids often bombard me with questions—'Why do I have to do the dishes? Can I go to my friend's house? Can I play the the X-box?'—and it overpowers me. I find myself thinking, *I don't know, I can't decide, I'm not decisive enough.*" So I coached her to first confide these negative thoughts to someone or something of her choice. Liz pictured her mother as her inner confidant and confided to her all of the negative thoughts traveling through her mind. Her mother reflected back to Liz saying, "You are a confident woman. You make good decisions all the time. You can be decisive with your children." "Thanks mom," was Liz's reply. She immediately began feeling confident in her ability to handle her children's parade of questions, and told me she was already feeling less stressed.

The tool of positive reflection is important for another reason. It has to do with what I call "psychic nutrition." When you feed on self–put downs, inside it's like you are eating all kinds of horrible, non-nutritive garbage. *I can't do this . . . I'm not like that . . . I don't have the patience . . .* This kind of thinking is totally toxic. Imagine picking up a rotting piece of meat and taking a bite out of it. You will wreak havoc on your digestive system. It's poison! Don't do it! But that is exactly what you are doing when you repeat the long litany of why you can't, don't, or aren't. Stop shoving the wrong stuff into your mind. Stop the diet of negativity. It will only discourage and hurt you.

I want to emphasize that the mirror is reflecting something that is accurate and positive about you. It is not saying, "You're the best parent in the world. You're a superhero. You can do no wrong." Those kinds of global statements are mindless ways of pumping yourself up artificially. Accurate and positive means the mirror is specifically zeroing in on something about you that it knows to be true, something already proven, something that you have forgotten because you were stuck feeding on all that negativity.

Hearing and receiving the positive reflection is a big step in correcting your psychic diet. If you want to be happy about yourself and robust in your parenting, start feeding yourself positive self-statements. It's like feeding your body healthy soups and salads. "I know I can be kind; I am happy; I do love my kids; I can say 'no' when necessary; I do listen."

Once you have started correcting your "mental eating habits," you are ready for the last tool to help you build your confidence.

TOOL #3: ENVISION THE STEPS TO CONFIDENCE

Confidence in parenting is the faith or trust in yourself that is built on what you do—on actions, not just on what you say. The third tool addresses the need for action. Such action must first take place in your mind. In other words, you have to see yourself doing what you thought you could not do. With this tool you will envision yourself being successful. You will cultivate an inner image that will help you think and feel better about yourself. You will use your imagination as the springboard to successful action.

Let's continue with our imagery exercise.

EXERCISE:
ENVISIONING THE SMALL, MANAGEABLE STEPS

Sit comfortably and close your eyes.

Breathe deeply and feel yourself connected to the chair and floor.

You have just confided your negativity in the confidant. The confidant has reflected to you accurate, positive things about yourself, and you have thanked it for that.

Breathe out and let the image of your confidant dissolve.

Now see and feel yourself taking a series of small, manageable steps to correct the original negativity.

Envision each small step in detail. See yourself taking each one successfully. It doesn't matter how small it is—what is important is that it is manageable and that you see yourself taking each one successfully.

Breathe out. Open your eyes.

What is this tool all about, and why is it necessary?

Confidence is built on knowing you can do something, and everything you do can be broken up into small, manageable steps. Look at how a baby learns to walk. First she turns over, and then, on all fours, starts to crawl. Next, she holds on and takes little steps. Finally, she lets go and starts to walk. This is the same process we go through with everything in life, even though we usually don't notice it.

Keep in mind this tool is not actually about taking the steps. This tool is about envisioning them—seeing them in your mind's eye—laying the groundwork. This is necessary because everything takes place in the imagination first. Look around you. Everything you see—the table, your chair, the computer, your clothes, the light bulb, this book—all happened in someone's imagination first, long before it became manifest in the physical world. It's the same thing with parenting. First, you must define in your imagination the small, manageable steps to succeed. Then you have to envision yourself taking them, one at a time, with your imagination paving the way.

Remember Liz? She was always feeling bombarded by her children's questions. After she received the positive reflection from her confidant she began to picture the small steps she would have to take to succeed at being more decisive. She closed her eyes, breathed deeply, and saw herself stopping whatever she was doing—dishes, computer work, laundry—to focus on her children and what they were asking. She imagined herself taking a deep breath, telling herself she can make a good choice, and making a decision immediately or telling her kids to come back in five minutes, so she can think about what she feels is best.

If you have a history of negative thinking, failing, or under-performing in any way, and then beating yourself up, you have to change your pattern. Envisioning these steps to your success is how your confidence will gain strength. What's more, positive images are like deposits in your optimism bank. The more you have saved up, the richer you are, and the more you have to draw on when something challenges you.

PERSONAL INVENTORY: TAKING STOCK

As we did in the last chapter, let's pause and take stock. This time we're looking at your productive and unproductive parenting habits concerning confidence. Habits related to confidence have to do with your thinking: what are you telling yourself about your parenting on a repeated basis? Taking stock will help you heighten your awareness, especially when you slip into an unproductive habit, so you can turn it around quickly.

Unproductive habits include:

- Frequent self-putdowns: *I'm a loser parent. I don't have what it takes.*
- Predicting a negative future: *I'll never be a good enough parent. I'm hopeless. I'm not going to even try.*
- Perfectionist thinking: *I have to do this perfectly, or I'll mess up my kids.*
- Frequent comparisons to others: *He works and still coaches his son's football team, I'm a loser. She cooks from scratch every night, I don't. Linda does so many fun things with her kids. I'm so boring.*
- Not speaking up for yourself because you're afraid people won't like you including your children: *If I say what I really feel everyone will think I'm not a thoughtful parent.*

Productive habits involve a different kind of thinking:

- Appreciating yourself for your good qualities: *I'm a good listener. I care about my kids.*
- Taking risks: *I'll give this a try. If I mess up it's not the end of the world.*
- Learning from your mistakes: *OK, I messed up. I see what I did wrong. I'll take care not to do it the next time.*
- Valuing your opinions: *This is important to me. I need to say something even if it's hard for my children to hear.*

The three Confidence tools keep you connected to the positive side of your mind so that you are self-supportive and encouraged. Your stress will go down, and your performance will go up. It's a matter of steady, determined self-effort and practice. Like anything good in life, you have to work for it. You become aware that your confidence is starting to slip, and you correct your course. You use the three tools before the stress becomes unmanageable.

Remember: no one wins saying, "No, I can't."

QUICK CHECK-IN: CONFIDENCE

When you are anticipating a challenging or stressful situation, or find you are in one:

Become Aware

- Are you feeding yourself negative self-statements?
- Can you identify them? Write them down.
- Breathe, ground, and sense (from the chapter on Calm).

Use the Tools

- Confide your negativity in the confidant.
- The confidant will reflect your positive qualities back to you. See the reflection.
- Envision yourself taking small, manageable steps.

Open your eyes and return to the present situation, staying connected in your positive, supportive mind.

QUESTION & ANSWER

Michelle: I have noticed that some parents are exceptionally negative about their parenting, to the point of deep depression. Are these tools enough to combat that kind of negativity?

Dr. B: I would look at the source of the negativity. I think that parents are fed, principally through the media, a non-stop stream of images about perfect parenting, and this produces a continual feeling of not measuring up. We live in a "comparison culture." We're always comparing ourselves to someone else, and usually we come up short, leaving us feeling like we're not good enough. Parents worry that they're not doing the best job and that the "mistakes" they make will have lasting, deleterious effects on their children. When we let go of the pressure of having to be perfect, we realize that learning from mistakes is a principal task in life. When we come to understand the greatest gift we can give our children is showing that we love them by what we say to them and how we act towards them, we realize we *are* enough, we *do* enough, and we *can be* enough just as we are as parents. We don't use the tools to *combat* negativity, we use them to transform negativity into its opposite: positive, growth-producing self-confidence.

In your question you said, "to the point of deep depression." If your bad feelings about yourself or your parenting persist or get worse, it might be wise to work with a professional confidant—like a counselor or clergy—someone trained to help you move through and transform these negative thoughts and feelings.

CHAPTER 7

How to Stay Focused

We're about to get into territory that's both rewarding and challenging, and I'd like to process a little with you on where we're going. In previous chapters, we've been working on your body and your mind. In the next chapter, we'll be working on your spirit. As you'll read in the pages that follow, "spirit" is a tricky word and a subject that is not usually or comfortably addressed. This is because, over the centuries, the word has taken on so many different meanings and connotations in countries and cultures around the world. Added to that, for most people, "spirit" falls outside of the world of science, which emphasizes what we can see and prove and tends to devalue, or even dismiss, what we can't.

As a performance psychologist I've come to recognize that spirit is a key element of the human makeup, and it is not tied to any one culture or country or religious tradition. I've seen—in myself and others—that spirit has a deep effect on how we handle challenges, how we deal with stress, and ultimately on how we perform as parents.

In working with you on the subject of spirit, I want you to know that I am not going to challenge your religion, your belief system, or your tradition, whatever that might be. And, if you don't practice in any particular religious tradition or subscribe to any belief system, I'm not going to suggest that you start doing so.

I do want you to recognize that spirit is the driving force for each of us. If you've ever felt charged up with anticipation about something, whether it's your child's big game, a visit to Grandma's, working towards a promotion, a date with your spouse, Christmas morning, or Chanukah lights, that's your spirit working. It's intimately tied into your goals—what you want for yourself as a parent—and what you do to achieve them. Your spirit is tied to your path through life.

In most of society we don't address the subject of spirit, yet I believe it drives and is the foundation of all of human performance.

WHAT IS FOCUS?

You're surrounded—an injured toddler, a shattered dish, an emotional teenager—all needing your attention at once. You're trying to make dinner, but it burns because you're busy bandaging wounds, cleaning up glass, and calming emotions. After ordering take-out, because dinner was a flop, you sit down to work on your PowerPoint for work the next day, but find you're not getting anywhere. You're re-running, over and over again, an argument you had with your teen, and you can feel her silent stare through the walls. Your toddler is crying for a bedtime hug, and you can see your partner out of the corner of your eye longing for a hug too. With so many things demanding your attention as a parent, how can you focus on anything at all? How can you be successful at reducing stress in such moments? How can you do what needs to be done at the right time and in an appropriate manner? Before you throw your hands in the air in desperation, let me ask you a question. In times such as these, where is your focus?

Focus is the third leg of our performance model—the three-legged stool. Of the three legs, Focus is unique, because without it you will not have lasting success in your attempts to improve yourself as a parent. You might ask, "How I can hinge the success of my parenting on the practice of staying focused?" When you're facing a challenging situation and you aren't calm, you can always hold your breath and tough it out. If your confidence is shaky, you can use sheer will power to blast yourself through. These two things are only possible, however, if you can focus on being calm or confident in such moments. You cannot in any way compensate for not having a goal or for becoming continually distracted. If you aren't focused—if your attention isn't pointed—your performance as a parent will suffer.

In May, when Dale looked at the yearly parenting goals he had made for himself back in January, he was disappointed. He realized he had not accomplished a single one. He liked the goals he had set for himself and was confident they were goals he could accomplish. So why hadn't he accomplished them? He wasn't focused on them.

What does it mean to be focused? Being focused means having goals that matter to you, staying on track, and consistently moving towards them. It's what successful parents do—they stay focused by connecting their actions to achieving their goals.

This, of course, is true of successful people in any field. Consider a brain surgeon who is removing a minuscule, life-threatening lesion from the left frontal lobe of a six-year-old child. She is calm and she is confident, but if she cannot focus she will not be successful. The surgeon cannot let her attention wander for a nanosecond since the tiniest lapse could result in her patient never speaking again. She is deeply dedicated to her work. She never loses sight of her goal. Every successful lawyer, dentist, artist, doctor, and parent spends years cultivating his or her skills. Whenever they stumble, which everyone does, they pick themselves up and get back on course. It is easy to make mistakes as parents, but from those mistakes you learn. This doesn't mean you will never make mistakes again or that parenting will suddenly become easier. It means you will become better and more prepared than you were before to handle your parenting stresses.

I asked my co-author, Michelle, what being focused as a parent means for her. This was her response:

> To me, being focused as a parent means being alert and present at the crossroads of my children's lives. Let me explain. A crossroad is somewhere a transition is being made—a place where a person goes from one place to another in order to reach a destination. As a parent I am the crossing guard at the crossroads of my children's lives. I don't walk across the street for my kids, but I am there while they do it, to make sure they make it safely across. This means that when my children come home from school, participate in recreational or extracurricular events, or are off to be with friends, I want to be there. I want to know about it. I want to be a part of their lives.
>
> Being focused also means following through on what I say. If I tell my kids I will be at their school talent show, I need to be there. Being focused means I avoid hypocrisy. If I tell my kids one thing I can't do another. Being focused means apologizing and getting back on track when I let my kids down in any way. All of this means that I am building strong, loving, lasting relationships with my children, and ultimately teaching them to be responsible and happy individuals, which is my goal.
>
> Real focus for me is keeping this goal at the front of my mind. It means planning and taking the proper steps to be at the crossroads—like organizing my schedule, knowing when my kids will be home and available, and being a firm support for my kids. It means when I fail, which I often do, that I get right back at it. Being a focused parent to me means having intentional goals,

being present, and ever willing to improve.

According to the dictionary, focus has a two-pronged definition. As a noun, focus is "the center of interest or activity." Think of the bull's-eye in the very middle of a dartboard. As a verb, focus means "to direct toward a particular point or purpose." Think of throwing the dart directly to this point. In regard to challenges in life, focus is also a noun and a verb. There is a goal of a successful outcome, and there is working toward that goal.

GOALS COME FROM YOUR SPIRIT

Being focused is, ultimately and intimately, linked to a very powerful source within you—your spirit. Your parenting goals might engage your body and your mind, but they originate in another part of you. Some people call this their soul, God, Goddess, or Higher Power. In this book, I will call it your spirit or highest purpose. Think of spirit as your power generator. It produces the energy that sparks every one of your achievements.

Throughout history, spirit has moved men and women to become great leaders, scientists, poets, musicians, athletes, and, yes, great parents. Mahatma Gandhi envisioned an independent India, and then secured it through a nationwide movement of nonviolence. Marie Curie hypothesized the existence of atomic properties and then discovered their structure. Mozart imagined glorious music and then scored stupendous operas. What about the mother who read to her child every day and taught her daughter a love of learning, leading her to pursue a life of teaching? What about the father who dreamed of being a part of his children's lives, and succeeded in building a relationship of trust and love so durable that the pattern of love and trust from father to child lasted through generations?

Your spirit expresses itself as your deepest goals and as the determination to do whatever it takes to achieve them. Spirit has the same Latin root as the word "inspire." It is *inspirare*, which means to breathe. I always talk about our goals as the way in which spirit breathes through us. When people, like those mentioned above, allow this to happen, we say they are inspired.

This is true for all of us. Think of a time when you had a goal that you were determined to reach and you worked doggedly toward it. Maybe you wanted to get a degree in sociology, spend more time with your kids, lose weight, build your muscles, or save money for a trip to Disneyland. Remember what it felt like when you were so highly focused? Chances are you felt enlivened, enthused, and satisfied.

Just having a goal however is not enough; you also need to keep working toward it. Focusing doesn't take the work out of work. But there is a payoff, and it doesn't just come at the finish line. During the process, you feel fulfilled, because you've got a goal and are fully engaged in achieving it, which means you are satisfying your spirit at every step. You just have to understand that your spirit is your driving force and learn how to stay connected to it. Then, whenever you are moving closer to your parenting goals, you will feel stronger and experience less disappointment.

The opposite occurs when you are cut off from your spirit. If you don't have a goal, if you're distracted from that goal, or if your goal is really someone else's, life feels far less manageable and much more aimless. This is often when disappointment and discouragement set in.

IS IT YOUR GOAL?

The first step to staying focused in your spirit is setting goals that are important to you. Developing your own goals as a parent is a process. When you're a parent, so much of who you are and what you do revolves around your children. Even when you do develop your own goals they often involve other people, specifically, your children and your partner—I want Devon to play on the accelerated baseball team; I want my husband to make more money; I want Leah to get good grades and go to a prestigious university; I want Dawn to have good manners. There is a problem with making goals like this. These goals require the direct participation of someone else.

In order to be successful in your goals there needs to be a shift. Your goals need to become self-driven. Ask yourself questions like: What do I want to do? What can I work at to make more money? What can I do to support my child in their chosen activities? What is my most important priority? What can I do to teach my child to love learning? How can I have better manners? How can I show my children I care? This means you are defining and pursuing your own goals.

Pursuing your own goals is not an act of selfishness. Unless a goal is yours, chances are you're not going to work for it, and the same holds true with your children. Think about it. If someone else is driving your agenda you might make a half-hearted effort now and then, but only when that person (usually your spouse, parent, or child) is nagging you. After a while, both of you are going to get tired of this scenario, and there will be a breakdown. You will feel resentful. They will be angry; you will lose interest and stop working. None of this is fun. If your primary reason for wanting to succeed at anything in your life is so that everyone around you will get off your back or do what you want them to do, you'd better return to the drawing board. Your drawing board. You have to want to succeed, for yourself as well as your children.

> Elaine was up to her ears in frustration. For years she had been trying to get her daughter, Shauna, to play tennis. She knew she would love it—eventually—and forced Shauna to go to practice every week. And every week, like clockwork, before practice there would be a blowout. "I don't want to go to practice! I hate tennis!" To which her mother would reply, "You are great at it, and I know one day you'll be glad you stuck with it."

It is obvious that Elaine needed to return to the drawing board and make a new goal. Her goals for success shouldn't hinge on her daughter's actions. If tennis is so important to Elaine, maybe she could sign up for a community class for herself. If her goal is to simply help her daughter to succeed, she needs to make a goal that helps her to support her daughter in her daughter's chosen activity.

WHAT ARE YOUR GOALS?

Let's consider your parenting goals. I suggest you consider putting them in three categories:

1. Day-to-day goals
2. Yearly goals
3. Life goals

Examples of day-to-day goals are: stay positive, spend time with each kid, be on time for work, have personal time with my spouse, eat dinner as a family, and go to bed by 10 p.m. A yearly goal might be: get out of debt, take a family vacation, or learn to speak Spanish. Life goals are those which move you forward on your path: to be around to enjoy my grandkids, to have the money to retire comfortably, to give more than I get, or to get through my bucket list.

Right now, let's work on your day-to-day parenting goals. This is a good place to start because when you learn to stay focused on your daily goals and enjoy the satisfaction of consistently reaching them, you will want to achieve your longer-range goals, and you will know you have what it takes to accomplish them.

Think about your life right now and write down three different parenting goals you have at this moment. They can be parenting goals that relate to one area of your life or three different areas (work, home, extended family), because being a parent affects every area of your life. Whatever they are, make sure they are yours. As you work through the next sections use your own goals to apply the suggestions I'll be giving to you.

EXERCISE:
YOUR GOALS

First, make a chart that looks like this:

My Goals	Mine?	Someone Else's?
1.		
2.		
3.		

In the first column on the left, list three of your day-to-day goals. In the middle column, answer the question: Is this goal mine? (Yes/No) If "no" and it's someone else's, list their name (My mom, My wife, My son) in the column on the right. For every goal you identify as someone else's, close your eyes, breathe out, and ask yourself, *What is it about this goal that I can make my own? What is it about this goal that I can make important to me?* When you've done that, open your eyes and continue to the next section.

Consider How You Are Going to Get There

Even the clearest of goals is just a starting point, not a delivery system. Attaining a goal is not like a hostile takeover. You don't say, "I will have a great relationship with my kid," walk into their bedroom and demand they tell you their deepest insecurities, secrets, and dreams. You've heard the old saying, "A journey of a thousand miles begins with the first step." For any goal, short or long term, you work your way toward your dream, one action step at a time. Maybe the first step in your goal to have a great relationship with your kid is going out for ice cream once a month just to enjoy one another or picking them up from school every day to have a little extra time to talk. Formulating your action steps in the right way makes facing the challenges of parenting less daunting.

Divide the Work into Action Steps: Make Them SMART

For many people, their goals seem large and overwhelming. Remember, any goal can be broken down into small, controllable chunks. These are your action steps. (And yes, they bear a direct relationship to the "small, manageable steps" you envision in the confidence tools.) What follows is a time-tested process for doing just that. It's called the SMART formula. When your action steps are SMART, they fulfill these criteria:

S	Specific	Your goal is precise and well defined.
M	Measurable	You can gauge whether you reached it or not.
A	Adjustable	You can adapt or modify it if you need to.
R	Realistic	Your goals are attainable given your available time, energy, and resources.
T	Time-based	Whatever goal you set is linked to the clock or calendar.

The whole purpose of this formula is to help you come up with action steps that are within the realm of the do-able so that you can really achieve them. It takes goal setting out of the "I wish" zone and puts it in the "I can" zone. You learn to plot the path to your goals in a way that isn't vague, grandiose, or unreachable. Instead, you will take steps that are precise, reasonable, and attainable.

An important tip: When you put your action steps into words, state what you need to do, rather than what you're not going to do—keep it positive. Negative steps sound punitive, and they don't really offer helpful directions—Don't be late! Don't waste the money! Don't interrupt! These will push your mind to rebel and say, *Don't tell me what to do!* A positive approach—Be on time! Save money! Listen!—makes you feel better and moves you along in the right direction.

Ted grew up in home with a lot of yelling. He had tried to change and do away with the yelling when he had his own kids, but he wasn't successful. After learning about the importance of creating positive goals, he decided that his daily goal would be to handle situations with his kids in a calm manner. I gave him the action sheet (below) and he filled out his action steps on the left-hand side. On the right-hand side is my evaluation as to whether the step is SMART or not.

Action Sheet for Ted

SMART = Specific/Measurable/Adjustable/Realistic/Time-based

Ted's action steps	Are they SMART?
Improve my patience.	SPECIFIC? As stated, this step is too general and not precise. Big, global, general steps usually feel enormous and overwhelming. They tend to paralyze rather than motivate. This step is not specific. What will Ted do to improve his patience?
Avoid the temptation to yell.	MEASURABLE? This is a vague statement that could mean anything. What if Ted doesn't realize the temptation even exists? How do you measure the "temptations?" This step isn't measurable.
Have quiet time every day from 7:00–8:00 pm to meditate.	ADJUSTABLE? While this looks like an admirable action step, every parent knows that unexpected events always intrude, even with the best plans. Right now this step is rigid and not adjustable. Ted is setting himself up for failure.
I'm always going to speak in calm, quiet tones.	REALISTIC? So far Ted's track record for yelling is frequent and consistent. Speaking in calm, quiet tones is not yet a habit for him. In fact, half of his communication could very well be categorized as yelling. Is it likely that Ted will never yell again? No. This step is not even a step—it's a big goal, and either way, it's not realistic. Ted is setting himself up for a big disappointment.

Take anger management classes for as long as it takes to kick the habit.	TIME-BASED? This might work if Ted had all the time and money in the world and nothing else to do but deep breathing. However, he has work, a family, and the rest of his daily life to tend to as well, and he can't keep paying for the classes forever. This step isn't time-based.

After Ted and I talked about his action steps in light of the SMART formula, he revised his action sheet. Here's what the new one looked like.

Action Sheet for Ted (revised)

SMART = Specific/Measurable/Adjustable/Realistic/Time-based

Ted's action steps (revised)	Are they SMART?
When my son Joey is defiant or ignores any of my requests, I'm going to take three deep breaths before I respond.	SPECIFIC. This action step is specific. It spells out in precise terms what Ted is going to do when his son is defiant, and Ted will be certain when he gets it done.
I'm going to keep a list of the things Joey does that upset me, so I can learn what triggers my yelling at him.	MEASURABLE. Ted is giving himself a clear yardstick for gauging his success. This step is measurable. If Ted records what upsets him, he'll be more aware and able to analyze what tempts him to yell. This will allow him to make the necessary changes. By creating this list, Ted is more likely to handle hard parenting moments in a calm manner.
Each day I'll review my schedule and plan for fifteen to thirty minutes of quiet meditative time during the day. I'll keep that meditative time in one chunk whenever I can.	ADJUSTABLE. This step allows for flexibility. Ted recognizes that quiet meditative time is important, and he's making this step adjustable to accommodate his varied schedule. (Of course, even fifteen minutes may require some downsizing when life is particularly hectic.)

Whenever I speak calmly with Joey as opposed to yelling, I will thank myself and tell myself, "Good job!"	REALISTIC. Ted's history of yelling at Joey to-date has been very numerous. In this step Ted is pushing to do a little bit better without putting too much pressure on himself, while being more positive at the same time. This is realistic. He is more likely to tell himself thank you and good job than he is to never yell again.
I will take one anger management class for six weeks and then re-evaluate the necessity of continuing.	TIME-BASED. Ted must balance the time he needs to take this class and the extra hours he's going to have to work to afford it with the rest of his obligations. By creating a time-based action step like this one, he will be able to accomplish his anger management objectives and still have room for his other commitments.

For every parenting goal you have on a day-to-day basis, make your action steps SMART. If you want to get to work on time, knowing the odds are against you—breakfast isn't ready, lunches aren't made, and you still have to drop the kids at the bus stop—it will keep you sane if you structure your time and set immediate goals that you can actually fulfill. SMART goals will keep your tasks sorted out, clear, and manageable.

Coaching you to use the SMART formula might feel like just one more task to add to your already brimming life, but I guarantee you that this is not a chore that demands more of you. It is a SMART template designed to make your life easier and more fulfilling as you accomplish small goals on the way to the big one of being a better, less-stressed parent.

DEALING WITH DISTRACTION

At the beginning of the chapter, I said that focus is a noun and a verb. We've just handled the noun, the point of focus, the goal itself. Now we have to work on the verb—the actions needed to reach the goal. If your action steps are clear, you know what they are. Taking the steps and staying on the path is another matter. Ella knows she has to put the kids to bed tonight, and she knows the sequence of steps that it will take—baths, pj's, teeth brushed, and bed time story. But what happens when it's actually time to start the bedtime routine?

I'll tell you what happens: either Ella does the work and gets it done— puts the kids to bed—or, she becomes distracted. Even with well-defined steps to follow, we all face the problem of distraction. You find out at 9:30 pm that your sixteen-year-old needs sugar cubes for his "Seven Wonders of the World" mural due tomorrow morning, the phone rings, your favorite TV show is on, or you're just wiped out. Becoming distracted is the biggest stumbling block to reaching any goal, whether it's a day-to-day, year-by-year, or a life goal.

For the Focus leg of the three-legged stool, distraction is Enemy Number One. It derails the momentum of that ongoing stream of actions that move you toward your goal. How often have you set out to achieve something and found that the day has gone by, and you spent it doing everything else but what you had planned, accomplishing nothing with your goal? You promised you would read with your seven-year-old, but you did the dishes instead. You want to peel the dinosaur stickers off the walls in your son's room, patch the holes, repaint, and decorate it to look more mature, but your sister called to update you on mom's health condition. You told your daughter you would take her to find a prom dress, but you decided to work late. You need to revamp the budget, so your kids can take violin lessons, but you watched YouTube videos instead.

Distractions are a direct manifestation of a disconnection from the spirit. If you look up the word distraction in the dictionary, you will find three different meanings with a notable interrelationship:

1. An obstacle to attention

2. An entertainment that provokes pleased interest and takes you away from worries and vexations

3. Mental turmoil, derangement

Doesn't this perfectly cover the process of being a distracted parent? First, your attention is diverted. Second, you kind of like it, because now you don't have to deal with your child's defiance, or at least you forget about it for a time. Third, there is a build-up of stress, because you've let so much time slip by without making any headway on your goal to improve your relationship with your son, so now you are anxious or depressed. What started out as a little blip in your attention span ends up as content for a therapy session.

Remember, distraction is your nemesis, and it will defeat you every time if you let it. If distractions are every parent's scourge—and believe me, they are—how do you conquer them? To put it another, more positive way, how do you stay connected and keep moving toward your goal? Simple. As we saw in the previous chapters on calming down and being confident you have to do two things:

1. Become aware, as soon as you can, that you are disconnecting, and

2. Use specific tools to reconnect and put yourself back on track.

CULTIVATE YOUR AWARENESS

The key is to crush the distraction before it becomes a mountain between you and your goal. You want to be able to cultivate awareness that you are becoming distracted as soon as you begin to veer off track. This is important because many people become distracted and they don't even realize it. Their mind is off and running, and an hour later they wake up and say, *Oh, wait a minute, it's early out day. I forgot to pick up the kids!* Other people know they're distracted, but they're in denial about it. They justify going off track by saying, "But I really do have to get that bid to my client. It wasn't a distraction from the kids; it was something that had to be done."

Jason told me he had carved out four hours on Saturday to take his kids for a hike and was thoroughly depressed when he came to see me on Monday. "We didn't get to go," he said. When I asked him to tell me what he did during those four hours, he listed these tasks: sleeping in, checking emails, fixing the closet, making breakfast, and pulling weeds in the garden.

It might seem unbelievable to you, too, that Jason gave into all these diversions, and that he was blissfully unaware of how unfocused he was. But believe me, in my thirty plus years of coaching people, I have seen this happen time and again. I have heard every conceivable distracting activity that parents engage in when they're supposed to be pursuing their goals: whether it be fixing the kids' toys, having date night with your spouse, or building a pinewood derby car with your son.

Here is a list of distractions I've compiled. These distractions aren't listed in order of rank, but they will give you some idea of what people are up against.

Dr. B's (Nearly) Definitive List of Distracting Activities

Which of these apply to you?

- Watching TV
- Playing video games
- Children fighting
- Watching YouTube
- Texting
- Going to a bar
- Doing laundry
- Organizing my desk
- Cleaning my room
- Cleaning the house
- Checking out Facebook
- Daydreaming
- Contemplating my life
- Shopping
- Eating
- Thinking about Christmas shopping
- Thinking about what to make for dinner
- Opening and looking into the fridge
- Tweeting
- Talking on the phone
- Checking my stocks
- Previous arguments with kids or spouse
- Going out for a drive
- Going to the movies

- Surfing the web
- Going to the beach
- Listening to music
- Throwing away old papers
- My kids homework
- Paying bills
- Messing with my iPod
- Cleaning out my wallet
- Filing papers
- Reading papers and magazines
- Job hunting
- My kid's friends
- Shopping online (eBay, etc.)
- Checking and answering email
- Going to the mall
- Worrying about money
- Going to the gym
- Thinking about going to the gym
- Shooting hoops
- Sick kids
- Playing with my pet
- Watering the plants
- Thinking about sex
- Having sex
- Volunteering for community or religious activities
- Tantrums
- Reading a book
- Making lists
- Complaining
- Wandering around because you forgot what you're doing
- Hobbies
- Taking a nap

Now add your own little specialties to the list. Do you need another page? Just kidding.

As you went through the list, you probably found points that made you stop and say to yourself, *Yeah, I did take a nap. But I needed to. A mom's gotta rest!* I understand—you need to do some of the things on the list—but not when you're supposed to be doing other things. Taking a planned break is quite different than drifting off and doing something else. If you persist in saying that you cannot avoid these little activities, ask yourself this: *Do I really have to go shopping right now? Is it worth missing my son perform the star role in* Into the Woods *to check the stock market? Am I just distracting myself because I don't want to talk to my daughter about her negative attitude?*

Often my clients call this "procrastinating." Procrastination is not something that is happening to you. It is something you are doing. It is a fancy word for distracting yourself. You are placing your focus on something else instead of on doing what you know you need to be doing to move towards accomplishing your goal. Focusing is all about where you direct your energy and where you train your attention. Procrastinating is about wasting your energy by training your attention on the unimportant.

Parents, more than any other group I work with, appreciate the importance of not procrastinating, because they spend so much of their lives trying to teach the principle to their children. Yet, like most people, parents often end up procrastinating.

Learn to recognize that losing connection to your parenting goals by engaging in distractions produces symptoms, the way sniffing and sneezing are symptoms of a cold. For example, Lee wanted to take his daughter out to buy a new dress. Just as his daughter and he were walking out the door he got a phone call. What Lee thought would be just a minute turned into an hour, and they never left home. Lee was so disheartened and upset at himself for becoming distracted. These symptoms tell you that Lee was disconnected from his spirit. Situations like this are the reason why it's so important to cultivate awareness that you are being distracted—because it is crucial that you stop and reconnect to your spirit and goals. Let's list some of the symptoms of distraction.

COMMON SYMPTOMS OF BEING DISTRACTED

- The distracting activity suddenly feels a lot more important than doing what you're supposed to be doing, say teaching your daughter about the birds and the bees.
- You feel too tired and drained to go on a date with your partner after spending all your energy doing other things.
- You are all jittery because in the back of your mind, you know the challenging situation—like bedtime—is still looming in front of you.

- Your mind is cluttered with thoughts that start with: *I can't handle this . . . I don't know how . . . and I'm not sure . . .*
- You aren't just anxious, but you are preoccupied with your anxiety.
- You are beginning to lose faith in yourself because, once again, you haven't followed through on what you said you would do. Perhaps you chatted too long with a friend instead of taking your child on a promised bike ride.
- Your kid(s) or partner is nagging you, losing faith in you, and questioning your motives.

What are your symptoms that tell you that you've become distracted? List them in your journal.

The awareness that you have grown distracted must come from inside you. If you are waiting for someone else to tell you to get back on track—perhaps your kids or partner—you are depending on an external cue. There are two problems with external cues: first, no one is going to be around all the time to monitor you; and second, when someone continually prods you (a spouse, child, or parent), you will likely feel resistant or angry. No one likes being ordered around, especially parents.

An internal cue, however, is entirely different. It is a thought or emotion of your own that contains the realization, *I'm distracted from reading a book with my five-year-old right now and out of focus. I need to get back on track.* And it is essential that you learn to point this out to yourself in a non-judgmental way, because if you put yourself down or talk to yourself in a threatening manner, then you will feel like you are being punished. *What's wrong with you? You are so lazy! She only wanted five minutes from you!* If you wouldn't talk to your five-year-old this way, don't do it to yourself. In other words, start looking at your negative self-talk, as we dealt with in the last chapter, as a distraction.

When you procrastinate, eventually there comes a time when there are no last minutes left and what you left to the last minute—often your children, concerns with your children, time with children, projects with children—are left undone or forgotten. If you haven't begun to manage your procrastination and distraction until now, it is probably ingrained. Deed has become habit, and habits have a way of lasting a lifetime—right into your children's lives, your home, and your relationship with your spouse and family members. When you procrastinate you are losing a bit of yourself and your relationship with those you love, because you are ignoring your spirit.

At some point, you will have to face yourself, your children, and your behavior and ask yourself, *If I go on like this, can I be the kind of parent I want to be? Do my kids look up to me? Do they even know I care? Do they know I listen?* You have to wake up to what you are doing, accept the fact that you are distracted from your parenting goals on a continual basis, and realize that it is working against you and your family.

This, then, once again is the first step—awareness. Unfortunately, becoming aware doesn't necessarily mean you want to change. You still need to answer the question: "Do I really want to stop distracting myself and start focusing?" Some people answer "no" to that question because being distracted isn't particularly unpleasant for them; in fact, they like it. When I asked one parent how she felt whenever her attention was averted from the task at hand, I expected her to tell me it was frustrating. Instead she happily answered that she felt great, "I'd much rather go shopping with my sister then stay home and listen to my kids cry, yell, complain, and tell me they think I don't love them because I asked them to scrub a toilet." For her, shopping with her sister was an escape and a much more peaceful alternative to following through with the kids. I told her, "Of course it's easier and more peaceful in the moment. That's not the point."

I asked her how she felt an hour before bedtime, when she reflected on how much she had procrastinated. How did she feel when she came home and the dishes weren't done, uniforms unwashed, her presentation for work still waiting for the finishing touches, and her children still needing her attention? Her mood dropped precipitously, "I'm always stressed, yelling at everyone, feeling like I'm on my own against the world, and feeling guilty that I spent all that time away from home and no time with my kids or spouse." And there we have it: it may feel good in the moment to avoid the stress with the kids or work that involves them, but the long-term effects are actually stress inducing, not stress relieving. This mother's habits of opting for the pleasant diversion instead of pressing forward was not going to change on its own. She had to want to transform them and work to do so.

THE THREE TOOLS FOR STAYING FOCUSED

So here's the good news: if you have a habit that keeps you from attaining your goals, and you are willing to work for a change, you are not stuck with the habit. You can break your old, unproductive habits, and you can establish new, useful ones by using the tools I'm about to give you. These tools may appear simple—and they are. Yet it never ceases to amaze me how often parents continue to engage in the same unhelpful, unproductive behaviors and patterns, and then feel frustrated and discouraged every time things don't work out.

Remember the physics principle, a body in motion stays in motion until it is met with an equal and opposite force? Well, it takes an effort equal to the force of the habit to stop its trajectory. You must actually do something different, not just try to stop what you have been doing. Simply stopping will leave a void. If you don't do something else instead, the old habits will automatically rear their ugly heads, fill the void, and spring back into action. What you need is a helpful step-by-step process of changing specific behaviors. Through repetition, this beneficial sequence will become your new habit.

You need to train yourself with the following three tools. That's all it takes—three. You simply have to use them consistently, with determination, and make them your own.

TOOL #1: STOP! LOOK AT WHAT YOU ARE DOING

Dean made a parenting goal to leave work at work and be home when he's home. It's Friday afternoon and Halloween weekend. He's tired. His son has called three times already wondering when he'll be home. Dean's ready to pack up his briefcase and leave the office, but he's got a few more memos to write and tasks to complete. After work he's planned to take his kids on a hayride and carve pumpkins. He's currently become distracted, daydreaming about the weekend. *I need to dress warm, I think I'll carve a Darth Vader pumpkin, I can just taste the apple spiced donuts and hot cocoa. The kids are going to love it!* When the phone rings, he is jolted back to reality and realizes it's thirty minutes to quitting time. How much time has he lost fantasizing about hayrides, pumpkins, and how Becky will scream all the way through the haunted corn maze? Now he either won't have time to send his last few memos, or he will be late for the hayride and disappoint the kids—again. Wouldn't it have been better if he had caught himself drifting off and said, "Stop! Wait a minute! The weekend hasn't started yet. My mind is off in the wrong direction."?

When you can do this—Stop! And Refocus—you stop the process of being distracted and stay in the present.

The following exercise will show you how to use the first tool and stop the distracting activity.

EXERCISE: STOPPING THE DISTRACTION

Sit comfortably in a chair, making sure your back is reasonably straight, and your neck and head are upright. Uncross your arms and legs. Rest your feet on the floor and place your hands gently on top of each leg. Breathe out and close your eyes.

Envision yourself having a goal. Let's say you have made a goal to follow through with your kids—if you say you will take them to the store, take them to the store, if you say you will read them a book, read them a book, etc. For example, imagine that right now you just told your son Calvin to stop texting on your phone and now you need to follow through and make sure he really stops.

See yourself working toward your goal. You see him holding your phone and imagine yourself watching him until he turns it off and hands you the phone.

Now see yourself becoming distracted. You turn to the computer to finish checking your emails and send a message to remind your co-worker about lunch tomorrow. *Where should we eat? I need to make an agenda for our meeting.*

Now, use the first tool, STOP! You see a stop sign, a stoplight, a hand goes up, or an alarm signal goes off. You stop the distracting activity (turning to the computer to check emails and send messages). As your hand goes to the keyboard, you realize, *I'm starting to go off track. Calvin is still texting and I have not followed through.* The urge to check emails and send messages is strong. You are thinking, *If I don't do it now I'll forget,* and then you think, *Does it really matter if he keeps texting? I just need to do this.* But you muster up a little discipline and focus on your priority: following through with Calvin. You tell yourself to *Stop.*

Once you have stopped the distraction, ask yourself the question, *Is this distraction going to help me reach my goal?* Is sending this email right now going to help me follow through with Calvin? Clearly, the answer is "No."

Open your eyes.

Stopping the distraction is the first tool. And stopping means stopping. It doesn't mean thinking, *I should stop,* once you are already off course and into the distraction. If you have a goal to do things with your kids that they love, and your daughters, Erica and Jamie, want you to play soccer with them, sitting on the couch tired and feeling overweight thinking, *I really should stop sitting here,* isn't actually stopping. You either get up and play, or you don't. Many people confuse the nagging thought, *I should stop,* with actually stopping. To really stop, you have to get off the couch and go play with your girls.

But why is it so hard to do this one little thing? Think of stopping as a battle between two parts of yourself: the adult and the child. The adult part—the part you try to teach your child day in and day out—understands delayed gratification, the meaning of work, the importance of putting in the time to build quality relationships, and foregoing pleasures until the necessary things are done. The child wants instant gratification, playing instead of working, spending time doing fun things, and receiving pleasure now, not later. Children are usually only interested in what is satisfying right now. The child inside you may want a big long pleasurable break from parenting. It might see the value in all the goals the adult has. It just doesn't want to work or sacrifice for them.

You cannot be a parent and a child at the same time. You are the parent, and your children need you to be their parent. They need you to face life's challenges. They need someone who will protect them, teach them, care for them, go to bat for them, spend time with them, be a good example to them, and love them. The adult part of you is the one who is expected to perform. Children sit back and expect to be taken care of. Unless you have perfect and unusually responsible children who don't need parents, you cannot afford to let the child inside of you take over.

Learning to *stop* yourself in order to improve your ability to stay focused is taught in virtually every spiritual tradition the world over. Why? Because these traditions, especially the ancient ones, have recognized for millennia the tremendous importance of owning your own attention by stopping when you become distracted. If you want to meditate, pray, become enlightened, be a good parent, understand the meaning of life, or fulfill your highest purpose—all goals of different spiritual paths—you must be able to control your attention. Unless you make a conscientious effort to stop becoming caught up in distractions and change direction, you will sink into a lethargic parenting inertia.

To recap, when you become distracted and unfocused use the first tool: Stop! And ask yourself, *Is this distraction going to help me reach my goal?*

The answer will be "No!"

TOOL #2: LISTEN

Stopping the distraction is only the first tool. You need a second tool that will redirect your actions toward your goal. The following exercise will introduce you to the second tool for staying focused.

 EXERCISE: LISTENING TO YOUR SPIRIT

Sit comfortably in a chair. Breathe in and out and close your eyes.

Envision yourself having a goal. It can be the same goal you were working on in the last exercise or a different one. Let's say it's to continue following through with your son Calvin.

See yourself working toward your goal. See yourself watching him turn off the phone and getting ready to hand it to you.

Now see yourself becoming distracted. Reading emails and typing messages.

Now use the first tool: Stop. You see a stop sign, a stoplight, a hand goes up, or an alarm signal goes off. You stop the distraction. You stop typing your message.

> Ask yourself the question, *Is this distraction leading me to my goal?* The answer is "No." You turn away from the computer. Breathe out.
>
> Now, use the second tool.
>
> Listen to the voice inside that's telling you exactly what you need to do to reconnect with your goal. Perhaps the voice is saying something like, *Go back to the couch where your son is still texting on your phone and follow through. If you don't take away the phone now, next time you tell him to do something, he's going to be less and less willing to do it, because he knows you won't do anything about it.*
>
> After you listen to the message inside of you, open your eyes.

The second tool is to listen and receive a specific inner direction. Literally, this means to tune into your inner voice. But when you first try listening, what you'll hear are a lot of voices back and forth—*You have to send the email. If I don't go to Calvin now he won't stop texting. People are waiting on you.* You need to think about what your goal is—following through with your son—and listen for how to connect to it, stay focused on it, and tune out the rest. Something inside you knows exactly what you need to be doing right now to achieve that goal.

Of course, getting Calvin to get off the phone isn't the most important thing in your life, but it is an important goal right now. As such it is connected to your highest self—your spirit—which is operating in even the smallest decisions that are made all along the way as you strive to meet your parenting goals.

Each one of us has this inner voice offering us helpful, explicit directions all the time. Imagine yourself with a little angel and devil perched on your shoulders whispering in each ear. This is what it is like. In that chorus of voices inside our heads, there are bound to be conflicting messages: *Man, I just want to sit here and watch football. If you go to bed now instead of watch football, you'll feel better in the morning, be more patient with the kids, and be on time for work.* Sometimes everyone seems to be talking at once.

I am well aware that some people say that they were listening to their inner voice, and then do things that are hurtful and destructive to their children and themselves. In its mildest form, the negative voice promotes bad habits. It tells parents to goof off and avoid responsibility. As it grows darker, it is the call to addiction, urging parents to drink, gamble, take drugs, be verbally abusive, and push away those they love and who love them. In its darkest form, it tells people to lie, cheat, steal, abuse children and spouse, and kill. This, quite plainly, is the voice of evil.

So how can you tell which one to listen to? You must recognize that out of this chorus, only one is connected to your highest self—your spirit—and it takes discrimination to tell which one. Here's a clue: The voice of your highest self always directs you toward that which is beneficial for you, your children, and others, never toward that which causes harm.

To prove which is the voice of your spirit, take the scientific approach. Try it out. If this direction serves to bring you back on track, then it is the voice of your spirit. If it drives you away from your focus, it's not.

After years of coaching people on how to meet their goals, I am convinced that every one of us has this voice and is the benefactor of its signals. Whether we listen to it and follow its direction is another matter altogether.

If you are having trouble grasping what this inner voice is, I'll give you a way of understanding it.

Remember how we discussed that the mind is like a talk radio station? Well your mind also has the ability to change stations, and it is constantly switching back and forth between stations. When you turn it on, you'll hear a lot of voices from the various stations, but only one of them is your own personal parenting radio station that broadcasts from your spirit. So which one is your station?

Here's what I tell my clients. First, take the initials to your full name and write them down in big capital letters on a piece of paper. Mine are BBB. What are yours? Write them in your journal. Next if you live east of the Mississippi put a W in front of your initials, and if you live west of the Mississippi put a K in front. What do you get? For me, I'm KBBB in California and WBBB in New York. What does that sound like? It's your own personal radio station. That is "the voice." It is your own private frequency, and it's always there to guide you.

When you set your dial squarely on your own frequency, you receive a good clear signal that tells you how to stay focused on what's important in your life, right now as a parent. It might be major—telling you to check with your doctor immediately about the unusual rash around your child's mouth; or it may be minor—prompting you to start applying for jobs closer to home so you can spend more time with the kids.

Usually, people think about the higher self as the part of themselves that deals with the mega-questions in life like, "Why am I here? What is the meaning of it all?" But life is made up of ordinary activities, and activities involve choices that will lead you in a certain direction—either toward your highest potential as a parent or toward a life of stagnation and disappointment. That's why it is so important to listen to your inner voice during all the little challenges, choices, and trials that come your way as a parent. Every decision you make either contributes to your growth and that of your child, or it takes away from your growth.

Listening to this voice isn't always easy. Sometimes we treat it like a snooze alarm—we let it wake us up for a moment, and then, as soon as the going gets tough, we fall back asleep and revert to our old ways.

I mentioned that it wasn't necessarily easy to listen to this voice. But why wouldn't you want to? Clearly it has your best interest at heart. Naturally, each person has his or her own unique resistance to it, but there are three difficulties I have found to be common to almost everyone.

The first is entitlement, and it comes in the form of, "Why can't I just do what I want to do? Why do I have to listen to this if it's telling me to take on hardships or to face a task with or for my kids that is frustrating and difficult?"

Second, there is the need to be in control. "I don't want to follow your guidance. Why can't I just do it my way?"

And the third form of resistance is apathy. "Why should I bother," the person says, shrugging his shoulders. "It's useless. My kid already ignores me." In all three cases, the parent is pushing the voice away and refusing to accept its presence, support, and guidance, partly because he doesn't recognize its importance.

What do people do when they don't like what the voice says? They start flipping the dial on the radio trying to find a different station—a "better" message. It is good to know, however, that even if you change stations, your spirit will keep right on broadcasting. You may not be tuned into it, but it will never leave you.

Whenever my clients fall prey to this kind of resistance, I ask them, "Who are you really fighting here? It's not your children." Invariably they realize that when they fight off listening to "the voice," they are fighting themselves. Again, this can relate even to the small things. Sometimes, late at night, when I'm on my way to bed and haven't brushed my teeth, my inner voice says, *You need to brush and floss,* but I respond with, *No, I'm too tired.* The voice tries again, and if I'm really grumpy I say, *Leave me alone! It's just this one time!* But after a few minutes I realize, *Who am I arguing with? Whose teeth are going to rot? If I don't take care of them, who is going to have to sit in the dentist's chair for hours and pay an enormous bill for the privilege?* That's when I listen. It is the question that makes me pay attention.

So how about you? When you don't listen to your inner voice telling you to apologize to your daughter for being impatient with her, telling the voice, "Leave me alone, she had it coming, if only she knew how easy she has it," who's going to hurt? Who's going to blame herself when her children won't talk to her? Who's going to pay the enormous bill for therapy? You are. Ignoring the voice won't make you or your daughter feel better. You will both continue to hurt or build walls to block out your pain.

The point here is this: when you don't listen to the voice of your spirit, you hurt yourself and very often your children. It doesn't matter if you like what the voice says. It does matter that you hear it and see the inner direction being pointed out to you without arguing with it or wishing it were different. Just listen. If you really do that one thing, you will recognize its value and appreciate that it is leading you to the right actions.

TOOL #3: FULFILL

Just listening to your inner voice is not enough. You have to follow through by heading in the direction it is telling you to take. In other words, take action in line with your highest self. The third tool then is this: fulfill your purpose by visualizing and then taking action on the message you've just received.

This is how I coach my clients to use this tool. This exercise reviews the first two tools and then introduces the new one.

EXERCISE: FULFILLING YOUR PURPOSE

Close your eyes and breathe in and out three times.

Imagine your goal: Following through with Calvin on the phone issue.

See yourself diligently working toward it. You are highly focused, and you feel enlivened and empowered.

Now you see yourself become distracted by a desire: You got some new emails, and you want to check them.

Immediately use the first tool: Stop! Look what you're doing.

Ask yourself: *Is this action helping me to reach my goal?*

Answer: "No. Calvin is going to hide in a corner somewhere and keep texting if I get distracted now."

Now use the second tool: Listen. Your inner voice is telling you exactly how to get back on track. What does it say? *Ignore the emails and go to Calvin. You told him not to text on your phone. Go follow through.*

Now here is the third tool: Fulfill. See yourself doing what the voice is telling you to do.

Open your eyes, and now do it. Act now. Don't give yourself time to resist. Take a deep breath, and remember why the goal is important in the larger scheme of things. If you don't follow through now, it will only be harder later. Now go to Calvin, have him turn off the phone and hand it to you. If he doesn't hand it over immediately don't give up. Follow through.

By reconnecting to your bigger goal, you place the desire to plan your luncheon and send your emails in perspective. It's just a momentary distraction that won't help you with your goal. A much deeper form of fulfillment will come from heading in the direction in which your spirit is sending you.

PERSONAL INVENTORY: TAKING STOCK

Staying focused is a big issue. We live in a worldwide web of distraction (pun intended): television, the internet, video games, junk food—you name it. And like the fly to the spider, you'll get caught in this web if you don't cultivate the necessary habits to stay focused. The pull to distraction in our culture is very strong. But the connection to your highest self is much more empowering and enduring.

Right now, take the time to do a personal inventory for yourself about your productive and unproductive parenting habits as they refer to your focus. As you read through the lists below, consider which habits you identify with.

Unproductive habits include:

- Not making a plan
- Letting yourself get distracted and staying distracted
- Abandoning your plan if you made one
- Putting things off until the last minute
- Knowing what you need to do, but doing the opposite instead
- Frequently blaming your distractibility on other people—like your kids—or events

Productive habits look like these:

- Making SMART goals
- Doing things on time
- Having a plan and staying with it
- Taking short breaks
- Considering what you want to achieve and owning those goals
- Taking responsibility for your actions

Focusing takes time, determination, and energy, but the payoff is big. You strengthen yourself, become a better parent, build better relationships with your children, and in the process make your dreams a reality. The Focus tools will serve you well time and time again.

Michelle shared a story about her mother:

When my mother started having children she gave up so much: her college degree, her time, and a career. She gave her whole self to her family with the ultimate goal to be the best mother she could be in the hopes of raising her children to be responsible adults.

There were literally thousands of setbacks to this ultimate goal. Not because she didn't care or wasn't trying, but simply because being a parent is hard. There is no formal training, there is always the element of the unknown, and your child ultimately will choose his own life and course. Here is what my mother said:

There was always fatigue because the only time I could ever get anything done was when my children were sleeping. When I thought I had things figured out, I would have another baby and everything would change. There were the days when I thought everything was against me. I didn't have money to buy school clothes. The house was a mess and the kids pretended like I didn't exist. I wanted to stay home with my children, so I worked from home as a piano teacher. There were hundreds of injuries to the kids, some minor, but some very serious. There were tantrums and tears, successes and failures—when my daughter hit her first home run, when my son received scholarships, when one of them had a one liner role in *Oklahoma!*, when one of the kids lost a student body election, or didn't make varsity, or all-state, I cried with them and for them. I laughed at them and with them. I taught them and disciplined them. It was a roller coaster ride. Every time we moved—and we moved often—it was a new adjustment for me and for every kid. Some loved it, fitting right in. Others struggled, being teased and made fun of.

There was teenage rebellion, and it stressed my relationship with my spouse, because I wanted to handle it one way and he wanted to handle it in another. Emotions ran rampant every day with someone or another, and every day we kept on keeping on. One foot in front of the other. I knew I couldn't quit when it was hard or freeze time when things were good. All I could do was focus on the ultimate goal, one step at a time, doing my best and learning to adjust when things weren't working. There was a lot of adjusting, a lot of learning, and a lot of saying, 'I'm sorry,' when I was wrong.

It took thirty years but the pay-off is huge. The day my youngest daughter was married to a good a man and each of my children, with their spouses, were there to celebrate, I cried. It was all worth it—every sleepless night, every discouraging moment, every distraction, every tear, every adjustment, and every sacrifice. My five children had happy successful lives. They were working good jobs, raising good grandchildren, married to good people, attending great universities. With the help of my husband and with my focus on my spirit, I did it. I reached my goal.

I'm still a mom. I still talk with my children, enjoy my children, and worry about my children. There are still setbacks and rough days. There are days when I miss them and wish they lived closer, and there are days I enjoy a bit of extra freedom. Being a parent never ends, but I'm so grateful I have seen such a great return on my investment. I'm glad I stuck with it.

Not every parent can devote themselves in the same way that Michelle's mom did, and they may not want to. However, every parent should have parenting goals no matter what their circumstances are. And whatever one's circumstances—single parenting, working extra jobs, poor marital relationships, or disabilities—every parent can devote themselves to their parenting goals. Too often parents let money distract them, success in careers, social networks, and a myriad of other things pull them away from those goals. Sometimes as parents you must give up something good for something you want more. So what do you want more as a parent? I understand clearly that sometimes just surviving is all many parents can do. However, when you make goals to succeed and you focus on those goals, like Michelle's mother, positive change will come about as your own successful story unfolds.

The great American philosopher, Henry David Thoreau, said it passionately in *Walden*, " . . . if one advances confidently in the direction of his dreams and endeavors to live the life which he has imagined, he will meet with a success unexpected in common hours."

As it says in an ancient, sacred text, "If not now, when?"

QUICK CHECK-IN: FOCUS

When you are anticipating or facing a challenging parenting situation:

- Define your goal (make sure it's yours!).
  - Specify the action steps you need to take to reach the goal.
- Become aware.
  - Are you becoming distracted into other activities?
- Use the tools.
  - Stop and look at what you are doing. Ask yourself, *Is this action getting me to my goal?* Admit that you are distracted.
  - Listen to the inner voice. What specific direction is it giving you?
  - Fulfill your spirit by taking the action that leads you back to your purpose.
- When you are in the challenging situation, become aware.
  - Notice that your attention is starting to wander.
- Use the tools.
- Again, stop and look at what you are doing. Admit that you are distracted. Ask yourself, *Is this helping me reach my goal?*
  - Listen to the inner voice. What specific direction is it giving you?
  - Fulfill your spirit and see yourself taking the action that leads you to reconnect with your goal.
- Open your eyes and take action.

We've just completed a major portion of the book, which is your training in becoming more aware of your body, mind, and spirit on your path to parenting success and fulfillment. Now you get to see how being calm, confident, and focused works in your daily life as a parent.

I'm taking a moment to pause here because I want to express appreciation to you for coming this far. And I want to strongly encourage you to keep going. It's one thing to read about tools; it's quite another to start using them.

There's an old Chinese proverb that goes like this:

> *I hear and I forget.*
> *I see and I remember.*
> *I do and I understand.*

Real learning comes from doing. With your awareness turned on, and your toolbox in hand, now it's time for the real learning to begin as you create more success for yourself as a parent.

QUESTION & ANSWER

Michelle: Dr. B, as a parent I have so many responsibilities with never-ending distractions that are often out of my control. When I have dinner on the stove and my two-year-old is climbing out the window after stripping down nude, I can't ignore that. He needs my attention immediately, but what about my burnt dinner in the kitchen? Even when I try my hardest, I can't take care of everything. I don't mean to put things off, it just happens. There are always distractions. What's your advice?

Dr B: At any moment, especially at a crisis point, you must ask yourself *What's most important that needs my attention right now? What do I need to focus on at this moment?* While your naked son was climbing out the window and dinner was on the stove, his safety was much more important than a well-cooked meal. A child's safety always trumps everything else. And yes, you have to accept the reality that distractions happen all the time. The issue is how you handle them: first you make a choice (what's most important right now?), and then you use the Focus tools to get yourself back on track. Also, you must accept that even with your spirit and goals in the right place, life is an ongoing process of challenges, and that you do the best you can, always committed to your own learning and growth. No one is perfect. Have compassion for yourself. Your focus, your goal, is to be the best parent you can be. And when you do all of this you are a great role model for your children.

CHAPTER 8

Using the Tools

LESS STRESS WITH YOUR PARTNER

She's so strict with the kids! There's no time alone. Who is going to stay home with sick kids? He never listens to my point of view! Does any of this sound familiar? Your partner is the love of your life. He or she is your other half. So why is there so much stress between you and your partner when it comes to raising the kids? There are so many reasons—different backgrounds, different personalities, and different passions. So what can you do?

We are not here to change your partner or make it so they don't stress you out. We have clearly covered the reality that you can only change yourself and reduce your stress. So how can you use the tools to have a satisfying and joyful relationship with your partner and be a successful parent at the same time?

COMMUNICATING CLEARLY

Communicating is key to your success in managing all stressful situations with your partner. You communicate with your eyes, your body language, and, of course, with your words. My goal is to coach you to have positive, productive communication with your partner using the tools—communication that helps you to be a better parent and enjoy your relationship.

David, father of two kids ages eight and thirteen, has just arrived home from his job as an accountant. He's had a bad day. He messed up on a large client's payroll, offended one of his co-workers, and he has a huge pile of numbers to crunch. He comes home, stomps past his wife and the kids—the eight-year-old waiting to play a promised game of catch, and his thirteen-year-old hoping for some help with math homework—goes into his home office, and shuts the door. His wife comes in to remind him of the promises he had made to his children, to which he responds very negatively. "Why do I have to take care of everything? Can't you help her with her math? I'm going to be working all night as is!" He was upset that his wife didn't just take care of things herself and he was feeling increasingly stressed as she lectured him on keeping his promises and being the kind of Dad his kids could trust. The next day, when David came for a coaching session with me, he said, "I just didn't want to deal with anyone. The kids just drain me, and my wife always makes me feel guilty about my not giving enough time to our kids."

From his perspective, his wife is always siding with the kids and reminding him of what an ineffective father he is. David feels he could manage with the kids if his wife would back off or support him, but he feels that, no matter what he does, it won't be good enough for her. So why try?

Try what? To change his wife's behavior? Some better communication might help, but there is no guarantee. It's David who has to change. "How?" he asks me, very warily, thinking I'm going to give him a dose of "Don't be so negative, your wife is right, and you have to sacrifice for the good of the family."

Since I'm coaching you, the reader, to be calm, confident, and focused, I want you to think through this situation with me, and what David can do to make a change.

A good way to start, in any situation, is to look at which "leg" of the stool could use strengthening right now. What would that be in David's case? Let's examine each leg briefly.

Calm. David is definitely not calm. He's had a crappy day and he's upset. Telling him to "calm down" or attempting to implement the Calming tools is probably not going to work right now.

Confidence. David is sure he knows how his wife will respond; he's confident in his assessment of the situation and that going right to his office and closing the door is, as he puts it, "the only way to go."

Focus. What is David's goal right now? Simply put: to be left alone. And what actions does he take to get to his goal? He gives his wife a silent *grrrr* and isolates himself in his room. David has repeated these actions so many times that they've become a habit. David's habit is, when I'm having a bad day, I shut my door.

David is not in tune with his spirit. We can know this because the voice he is listening to is not helping him improve or become a better father. It is telling him to retreat. As we've been working together, we've looked at productive and unproductive habits, and through that lens I'd say his habit of retreating is unproductive: it doesn't lead to any positive outcome, and it ends up in disconnection. Remember, disconnection is the root cause of stress. At this point David said, "But my wife is the problem. She doesn't listen to me, and she doesn't understand the pressure I'm under, so what else can I do but close the door?" Expecting that his wife will change is not going to work. So what can David do? He can do something different. He can use the tools to communicate clearly.

Here's what the same scenario would look like if David used the tools.

David has had a bad day—the payroll, the co-worker, the number crunching—and he comes home in a bad mood. Rather than have his goal be isolation, stomping through the house, and locking himself in his office, he can take on a different goal: to communicate clearly. With this goal he takes the following action: he sits down with his wife and says, "I've had a bad day and before you say or ask for anything I need twenty minutes to unwind."

You may well ask, what happens if David goes through all this and his wife gets upset, "You never keep your promises with the kids, and I have a job, too! When do I get a break?" Sure, David might want to stomp up to his office, shouting, "Big surprise! I knew she would be mad and unreasonable. That crazy Dr. B! What was he thinking?" Or, he could use the tools.

The first one would be the Calming tool of breathing. When something is happening outside of you that you don't like, one of the first things you disconnect is your breath. You just stop breathing without even realizing it, your blood pressure goes up, and you want to scream, or you want to get out of there. So breathing is first, and then quickly grounding (that will keep David there with his wife and kids, not stomping away). He might even use sensing by looking at the bigger picture: actually seeing his wife's desire for him to be with the kid's as a sign of her integrity and desire to do what's best for the kids. Maybe realizing she is tired, too, and that tomorrow will be a new day at work.

In this calm state, David can say to his wife, "When you get upset with me about the kids I don't enjoy it. It makes me want to hide in my office. I love you, and I do want to be with you and keep my promises with the kids. I need you to be patient with me when I have a bad day, just like you need me to be patient with you."

This is a clear communication. It starts with Focus—the goal is to stay connected and to take actions that get you there. In David's case it would be talking to his wife instead of running away and being upset when she came to "lecture" him: staying calm, and working things out together instead of feeling and acting that it's hopeless and things will never change.

Where does the confidence leg come in here? Let's run through how to use those tools in this scenario. I ask David to close his eyes and look into a mirror and see his best, most productive, and highest self and tell me what he sees. "I feel strong, I'm smiling. I feel good about myself, my job, and my family." Now I coach him, standing at the mirror, to see himself using the Confidence tools. First, he must confide in the image in the mirror, tell it the negativity (and remember this has to be a negative feeling about yourself, not someone else). David says, "I don't have the patience to communicate with my wife." The mirror then reflects back something accurate and positive. For David it's, "You've stayed calm and reasoned with your wife before. You can do it."

Now David envisions the small manageable steps he can take to correct the negativity. He sees himself changing his goal—to communicate clearly—then he sees himself using the Calming tools—breathing, grounding, and sensing— asking his wife to listen, and then telling her that her anger and over persistence makes him want to hole up in his office. After this, David opened his eyes and said, "It's true. I can communicate with my wife. I can ask her to listen. I can stay calm even if she is upset."

Communicating clearly with your partner means two things:

1. You say what's going on with you.
2. You say what you need from your partner.

After that, it depends what kind of relationship both parties want. In David's case, his wife did want a better connection with David and she put in a great effort, not to nag, but instead to support him and try to understand his struggles. Neither David nor his wife was perfect in their efforts, but David continued to communicate with her in clear consistent ways.

My hope for all partner relationships is that both partners would want to keep improving their connection and help it to grow (remember, better connection means less stress and better performance, in this case, as a parent team). Sorry to say, that's not always the case. You might want a better relationship with your partner, but they may not be willing to work at it. So, again, you have to do what you can which is to communicate clearly.

Remember, shutting down doesn't help. It's a disconnection, and it per-petuates the stressful feelings. Sure, you may get angry and need to shut down for a little while till you can calm down and reorient your focus (use the tools!), but once you've made those adjustments, get back into the re-lationship and communicate clearly. Also, people can't read your mind. If you shut down you are likely expecting that others will just know how you feel. Most often they don't. They are busy dealing with all their own stuff. Take responsibility for yourself, stay connected, and communicate clearly.

RESPECTING DIFFERENCES

David learned what he needed to do to communicate clearly. But commu-nicating is a two way street. It also involves listening to the other person and responding to what they have to say. When you respond, you need to be respectful of your partner and how they might be different than you are.

Erica, and Ken are not getting along. Their daughter didn't do the dishes when she was asked to. Erica tells her she can't go out with her friends. She goes to Ken in tears. "Mom won't let me go over to Rachel's. We've had this planned all week. I had so much homework and school activities, I just didn't have time to clean up." Ken, with all of his compassion, (which Erica usually loves about him) tells Erica, "It's not that big of a deal. You are too stern. She just didn't have time. I told her she could go."

Suddenly Erica's stress level is soaring. Her heart rate increases, her face gets red and hot, and her ears ring. She is thinking (or maybe yelling), *I told her she couldn't go, and you need to support me!* Erica feels like this situation is a constant losing battle for her—feeling like her daughter has Ken wrapped around her fingers. Erica's thoughts are becoming negative. *I'm not appreciated. I can't do this. I'll never get through to my kids when my husband won't support me. I care about our daughter just as much as he does. I want to talk to him, but I'm not sure it would make a difference. I just don't know what to do.*

In coaching Erica, I tell her she was off to a good start: thinking of what she could do, rather than trying to change her partner. Erica was certainly not calm when Ken did not support her in the discipline she gave to their daughter. And she was not confident that things would change with Ken. This leaves us with the Focus leg. Let's review what Focus is all about: having a goal and taking actions to get to it. In discussing this with Erica, I ask, "Erica, what's your goal with Ken?"

"To get him to back me up, support me, and listen to me when I discipline our daughter."

"No," I say, "you just slipped into changing-someone-else-mode."

She takes a moment to think. "I guess it's to have unity with Ken when it comes to discipline with our daughter."

"Exactly," I say, "let's see what actions can take you to that goal."

I coach Erica to get together with Ken and to use the dialogue.

Erica says, "Ken, I'd like to talk with you. I'm not sure you want to talk with me, so I'm going to suggest we have what Dr. B calls a dialogue."

Ken timidly agrees, assuming it's going to be a lecture.

Erica continues, "Here's what I'd like us to do. I'm going to start by telling you what I want for our relationship and what's bothering me about it. I'm going to focus on my feelings, not on telling you what to do. I would like you to listen. When I finish you're going to repeat what I said. Then we're going to switch it. You're going to tell me what you want and what's bothering you, and I'm going to listen and then repeat what you said. Can we do that?"

Ken agrees.

THE DIALOGUE SETUP

The setup of the dialogue is very straightforward. First, you get the other person's agreement to talk, and then you explain the ground rules:

1. When Person A talks, Person B listens without making comments, criticisms, or asking questions.

2. Person A talks about himself, not about the other person. He uses "I" or "me" statements like, "I feel put down when you say, 'You're such a control freak,'" (rather than, "You're wrong for putting me down.").

3. When Person A is done, Person B repeats exactly what he (or she) heard.

4. Then you reverse the process.

Let's see what happened with Erica and Ken when they did this:

Erica: I would like us to have more unity in our discipline.

Ken: You would like us to have more unity in discipline.

Erica: I feel frustrated when I give our daughter a discipline and you change it.

Ken: You feel frustrated when you give our daughter a discipline and I change it.

Erica: And when you do that, I don't feel supported.

Ken: And when I do that you don't feel supported.

Then Ken gets his turn.

Ken: I feel protective of our daughter when you discipline her over things I feel are unimportant.

Erica: You feel protective of our daughter, when I discipline her over things you feel are unimportant.

Ken: I feel bad for our daughter because she has so much going on at school. I would like it if we let up on her sometimes.

Erica: You feel bad for our daughter because she has so much going on at school. You would like it if we let up on her sometimes.

Ken: It would mean a lot to me if you asked me my opinion on how I feel we should discipline our daughter.

Erica: It would mean a lot to you if I asked you your opinion on how you feel like we should discipline our daughter.

Ken: I'd like more unity on discipline, too.

Erica: You'd like more unity on discipline, too.

What's happening here? The dialogue gives Erica and Ken a structured and safe structure for each of them to express their feelings and know they are being heard. When a person mirrors back to you exactly what you said, you know they "get it."

In the dialogue the two people don't accuse or blame one another. Each person states what's going on for him. The format ensures that each person will have a chance to speak and to be listened to without comment or criticism.

Some years ago, my wife and I were having trouble communicating. Anything either of us said got under the other person's skin so quickly that any remark was like lighting a short fuse that immediately triggered an explosion. Talk about an unproductive habit! We knew we needed help. The counselor we went to coached us to have a dialogue. Then she said, "The mark of a good relationship is that each person holds what the other person thinks and feels with equal weight as their own feelings." This isn't easy. We're very quick to think, *I'm right, and the other person is wrong.* The real deal is *I feel this way, she feels that way. Her feelings are just as right as mine are.* In fact, there's no such thing as a "right" feeling because that would imply there's a "wrong" feeling, and no one's feeling is wrong; it's simply his or her feeling.

Just as you want your partner to respect you—your thoughts and feelings and ways of looking at things—you need to respect them. A climate of mutual respect for each other's differences means less stress, more acceptance, and better performance as parents.

What tools are we using in the dialogue? Certainly the Focus tools: we have a goal (to have a better relationship), and the dialogue is a sequence of actions that take us to the goal. The Calming tools also come into play. When you listen to the other person you don't flare up, scream, or run out of the room—you listen. And while you're listening you can use the tools of breathing, grounding, and sensing.

And confidence? Ultimately, confidence is built on taking small, manageable steps successfully. That's just what you and your partner are doing together when you go through the dialogue step-by-step. By having the dialogue, you are building your confidence in yourselves ("I can say what I need to say."), each other ("We can listen to each other."), and the relationship ("When we respect one another we have a better relationship."). Remember, the word "confidence" means "trust, loyalty, and belief in." The dialogue is a process of building mutual respect, and by doing so, you trust each other and believe in your possibilities together.

One more thought here. You'll notice I haven't said anything about agreeing with each other. This isn't about agreeing. This is about really hearing one another and respecting how the other person is different from you. If you have the expectation that your partner should agree with you, please let go of it! Because that means you're thinking, *I'm right.* Well, guess what? Everybody's thinking that! So let's get a new baseline going: "I have my feelings, thoughts, and reactions just like everyone else has theirs." That's called mutual respect. When you have to come to an agreement on some matter—whether it's discipline, household work and parenting responsibilities, time with your spouse, or scheduling concerns; whether it's your child's curfew, or their allowance, or their diet—communicating clearly and having mutual respect will go a long way to finding a solution that works for both of you and having a relationship that is healthy and enjoyable.

A MESSAGE FOR THE SINGLE PARENT

If you're a single parent your stresses are magnified and multiplied. You have to do everything on your own: you work to support the family, cook the meals, wash and fold the laundry, deal with your ex-spouse, go to parent-teacher meetings, take care of family finances, discipline the kids, and on and on and on. And all of this by yourself.

Using the model to be calm, confident, and focused, may seem unrealistic——a dream that will never come true. You might well be thinking, *I'll never be calm, confident, and focused. I'm too stressed out!*

This is called "black and white thinking." It sounds like there are only two states of being: (1) being stressed out or (2) being calm, confident, and focused. The truth is, it's never one or the other; it's both. Life is a changing, developing story. Your stress level fluctuates from day to day, and even on a single day you'll experience moments of more stress and less stress.

So how can you, as a single parent with so many responsibilities, handle all the stresses in a better way?

First: realize you are not perfect. Just as your children are learning and growing, so are you. This means you're going to mess up sometimes (you start to yell; you feel like you're a failure; you're too distracted to get anything accomplished). Rather than beat yourself up (*I'll never get this right.* or, *I'm a bad parent!*), you cultivate your awareness and use the tools.

"Cultivate your awareness" means you pay attention to your internal cues when your stress level starts to rise (your heart is racing, your face flushes, your negative inner voice gets louder, your attention wanders), and then you "use the tools," which means you use one or more of the nine core tools to calm yourself down, build up your confidence, or stay focused.

In this way you are doing what you can. You affirm this to yourself by saying, *This is what I can do. I'm not perfect. I'm trying.* With this practice and attitude, you'll accomplish three things: (1) You will move yourself into a different place (to be a little calmer, more confident, and more focused); (2) You'll appreciate yourself for what you were able to do (rather than beat yourself up for what you weren't doing); (3) You're showing your kids that life is about handling challenges as best you can—not about being perfect.

Next: the most important thing for a single parent to practice is showing your kids that you love them. Sometimes this is hard when your stresses are all piled on top of each other and when your children keep adding to the pile (not liking anything you cook; keeping the house or apartment a mess; "forgetting" to call you when they stay out late). Without the assistance and sometimes the buffer of another parent, when your kids are with you, you are their source of sustenance, love, and support. No matter how stressed out you may become, always return to the love you feel for your children. Then make it a point to express that love. By giving a hug, a kind word, a little note or email, you're sending your children the message that they are important, that stresses come and go, and that what endures is love.

Lastly: as a single parent you need support. Whether you get this from extended family, your friends, the people at your church, synagogue, mosque, or community center, you need to get it from somewhere. We all need the support of others. We rely on human interaction for the care, empathy, and love that is part of the basic fabric and fuel for living. With the mushrooming growth of the web and internet, online communities of single parents are sprouting up all over. Put the words "Single parent support group in _____ (name your community)" into your search engine, and you'll be surprised at what comes up. You are not alone.

Remember: stress is a function of disconnection. You are doing everything you can for your children. You are staying connected with them in so many different ways on a daily basis. But you need connection too. When you meet and befriend other single parents who are facing the same tests, challenges, and stresses that you do on a daily basis, you will experience great relief. Remember: you are not alone.

TAKING CARE OF YOURSELF

A complete night's rest becomes a dream in and of itself—that's what happens when you have toddlers. There's no time to read that book that's been sitting on your nightstand for months or watch your favorite team play—that's what happens when you have kids. There's no hot water left for your shower so you either go without or go cold—that's what happens when you have teenagers. There is just something about parenting that exhausts every part of you and provides you little time or opportunity to rejuvenate.

The problem with this is that you cannot be in your optimal zone of success as a parent when you have no energy. Being calm, confident, and focused requires work, and work requires energy. Now is the moment many parents laugh, "You can't be serious Dr. B. I have no extra time for myself, and when I do, I give it to my kids." I'm not here to help you find more time. Everyone has twenty-four hours in a day. The most productive people throughout history also had 24 hours in a day. So what made them so productive? They had productive habits.

Your kids aren't going to stop needing you, your energy, your love, or your time. So, what can you do?

PRODUCTIVE AND UNPRODUCTIVE HABITS

Throughout the book we've been looking at your productive and unproductive habits: habits that help you reduce your stress and keep yourself calm, confident, and focused; and habits that disconnect you and keep you stressed out. Taking better care of yourself means cultivating productive habits. Look back over the lists in Chapters Five, Six, and Seven and determine how you can move yourself in the direction of building productive habits for yourself.

Here's Adrianne's story:

> Adrianne had just taken on a new job and also decided to become more active in her political community. The little bit of time she used to have for herself and her kids was disappearing. She would labor late into the night trying to get caught up on work. This was after she had already spent her evening making dinner, cleaning house, doing laundry, taking kids to cheer practice, and helping with homework. Weekends were about the same. No time for

herself. Night after night she stomped around her children in a state of pure drudgery. Anything that went awry would send her stress levels soaring. Sometimes she could keep her emotions in, but inside she was falling apart. Thoroughly exhausted and physically sick, she broke down, "I just can't do it all. I want to be a good mother. but I don't have the time."

Adrianne was outwardly calm with confidence that if she had a direction to take in improving her parenting and her happiness, she could do it. We decided it would be best to work on the Focus leg. I suggested she make a goal for herself using the SMART steps we discussed in Chapter Seven. I reminded her that if she wanted more time to take care of herself she would have to change something in her life. She would need to do away with some of her unproductive habits and replace them with productive ones. She thought of some of her unproductive habits—skipping breakfast, working late into the night, and an unorganized schedule. Instead of just saying she would not work late anymore, she decided to make a more productive and decisive goal.

Exercising each day became a goal for Adrianne. She felt she should have been doing it long ago. It was time to listen to her spirit. She knew it would give her more energy for parenting and help her feel better physically. The goal was set. Now it was a matter of following through.

She also acknowledged her evenings were filled with work, keeping her up late into the night. She knew her tired mornings and short patience were unproductive. An earlier bedtime would give her more energy to exercise and would reflect the kind of aura she wanted for her children. Another goal was set.

As a parent, like Adrianne, you need to create habits in your life that give you time to take care of yourself—habits that rejuvenate you and help you be the best parent you can be. If you're skipping meals to surf the web, focus on a habit that will satisfy you and improve your abilities as a parent. If your schedule is disorganized and you are wasting time or feeling frazzled, focus on using a calendar or taking a class on organization.

I often hear from parents, especially mothers, that they feel guilty taking time for themselves or spending money on themselves. It is your responsibility as a parent to take care of yourself. No one can do it for you. Your children need you—your best you.

TEACHING THE TOOLS TO YOUR CHILDREN

We have discussed how using the tools to being calm, confident, and focused can help you be successful as a parent. Now let's discuss how you can teach these tools to your children to help them find success in their own endeavors. These tools will help your child handle any challenge life throws at them, whether it's at home, at school, on the playground, or as they grow into their adolescence and young adulthood. In other words, you are giving them a foundation for their own growth.

There are three critical aspects to teaching your children about the tools and how to use them.

The first is that you are their model. Children learn by imitation. They watch and listen to what their parents say and do, and they repeat those actions. Second, as a parent, you are your child's first and, I would say, most important teacher. And third, as a parent, you are facing stressful situations every day—some that involve your kids, and some that don't. Your son falls off his bike and cuts his leg requiring a rush to the emergency room; you get a call from your bank that your account is overdrawn; your spouse is having a bad day. There's no end to the possibilities and combinations of the challenges a parent can face in a single day.

Your children are very attentive to how you deal with the stressful situations that come your way. They're aware of how you respond to stress for two reasons, which may not be at all conscious to them: (1) They want to see what you do: does mom have a meltdown, or is she able to calmly work through the issue? and (2) They want to know how your reaction is going to affect them. If you get angry about your neighbor making noise in the middle of the night, how will you act towards them (your child or children)?

Let's establish an important tenet about modeling before we go further: you are not perfect. You can't be calm, confident, and focused all the time in every stressful situation. Sometimes you may lose it. And when you do, and your child witnesses that, what becomes important is how you recover and what you do next. Here's a story to illustrate the point.

> Steve, father of eight-year-old twins, took the boys out for a bike ride in the hills behind their home. It was a clear, crisp, somewhat blustery day. The boys, Evan and Jack, each on his own bike, were quite different in bike riding skill. Evan, like his dad, was pretty fearless and could handle rocky, rough terrain. Jack, on the other hand, was much more cautious to the point of getting frightened when the road got rocky. When they came to a challenging part of the trail Steve and Evan forged on but Jack slowed down and eventually stopped. Steve got frustrated. "Come on, Jack!" he yelled. But Jack had come to a standstill. He just stopped. It was getting late and darkness was settling in. Steve was worried that they wouldn't get home while there was still enough light to see. He pedaled back to Jack. "What's the matter with you?" he asked. His tone was angry. Jack started to cry.

> At that moment Steve realized that he'd lost it. He wasn't even thinking about being calm. As soon as he became aware of his own stressed-out state, he used the calming tools. He took a deep breath, felt the ground under his feet, and opened his senses to see that he had one scared little boy on his hands. He considered what the goal was at that moment. To get the kids home safely before it gets dark. With this focus, and in a much calmer state, he said, "I'm sorry, Jack. I just blew it. You got scared because the

road got too hard for you." With Evan there, they considered their options, and decided it was better to backtrack to the smoother ground, rather than press ahead and make matters worse for Jack.

Modeling the tools for your children means letting them observe how you use the tools when you are stressed. Steve let the stresses of the late hour and a scared child get under his skin. He was angry, but then, as soon as he became aware of what he was doing, he immediately recovered by using the tools to reduce his stress level. Not only did this make a difference for Jack, who was also able to calm down, but it was important for his brother, Evan, to see that their dad could make an error and then recover.

You can reflect on a situation and how you are handling it as the situation is going on (as Steve did above) or after, when things have calmed down. The message that you're sending to your children is that life is filled with stressful situations, and when we respond in a more calm, confident, and focused way we'll insure a better, more productive outcome.

The second aspect in teaching your children about stress and using the tools is to sharpen their awareness of the stressful situations they face on a daily basis and what they can do to reduce their stress. One particularly helpful way to do this is before a stressful event occurs as Mary Jane did with her daughter, Eliza. Eliza was nervous about a presentation on crickets that she had to give to her middle school class. She had done all the research and prepared a couple of good posters, but she was worried. She told Mary Jane, "The teacher isn't going to like what I've done, and the other kids aren't going to listen."

Mary Jane responded to Eliza by saying, "I see you're worried, and I understand your concerns. I know you've done really good presentations before. Let's see what you can do calm down and do a good job tomorrow."

Notice that Mary Jane was directing Eliza's attention back to herself. Eliza can't change how the teacher and children react, but she can work on herself. This is a basic building block for the model offered in this book. You can help your child recognize that if she's feeling stressed she is disconnecting from what she needs to do to stay calm, confident, and focused.

In Eliza's case, her disconnection happened because she was putting her focus on the teacher and her classmates. Mary Jane helped Eliza reconnect by reflecting back to her daughter that she had confidence in her ability to do a good job based on her past performance. Then she worked on getting Eliza to envision the small manageable steps she could take to do a good job in class. Eliza could see herself presenting each point clearly, letting her own natural interest in the subject shine through as she spoke. Mary Jane added a dollop of the calming tools by teaching Eliza how to integrate breathing and grounding into her presentation by suggesting, "Each time you finish a point, let your breath out and feel your feet on the floor." The net effect of this interchange was that Eliza became more aware of her own stress (getting nervous) and then had specific tools to reduce the stress she was experiencing. The presentation turned out to be clear, and Eliza got good feedback for it.

The third way you teach your child about stress is to offer him a safe place to review and evaluate how he handled stressful situations during the day, at home, or at school. Susan did this with her son Sam. Sam is a first grader and Susan heard from Sam's teacher that he was in a big argument with another child, Josh, over who could use a special toy in the play corner. "It was my turn!" said Sam, justifying his outburst. "Josh played with it, and he wouldn't give it to me." Susan reviewed the situation with Sam, asking him to close his eyes and see what happened when Josh wouldn't give up the toy.

"I was mad," Sam said.

"What happened then?" Susan asked.

"I took the toy away from him," Sam replied.

Susan took it a step further. "Now, let's look at the whole thing again, in a new way. See Josh playing with the toy. You know that it's your turn, and you feel angry, because he's not giving up the toy. Can you see that?" Sam nodded. Susan continued, "But instead of grabbing the toy you take three deep breaths, real deep ones, down to your belly to calm yourself down." Sam did this. "Now," Susan continued, "imagine walking over to Josh and saying in a calm voice, 'Josh, it's my turn to play with the toy now.'"

"But he still won't give it to me!" Sam quickly shot back. This gave Susan the opportunity to discuss alternatives with Sam about how he could achieve his goal (playing with the special toy): Sam could talk with the teacher and ask her to intervene, or he could tell Josh he'd like to start playing with the toy in five more minutes.

Notice that Susan didn't say, "You should be more patient," or "Everyone has to have a turn."

These type of responses sound like lecturing, and children turn off when you start talking this way. Your child wants to make sure that you understand why he got angry and be sympathetic with his situation. It's best that you mirror your child by saying, "It makes sense you were angry. It was your turn," and follow up with options for action the next time he's in a similar situation.

Remember, your goal is to cultivate his awareness of when he feels stressed and to give him tools to react in a more productive, less-stressed way.

You also want to teach your child not to blame someone else when he (your child) has an emotional reaction. Sam exploded when Josh wouldn't give up the toy and said, "Josh made me angry!" Susan's reply to this was, "You didn't like what Josh was doing. You wanted him to do something different. When he wouldn't do what you wanted him to, you became angry."

Teaching your child to take responsibility for his own reactions and feelings is an important part of teaching him to use the tools to reduce his stress. Saying, "I'm feeling angry," is very different than grabbing a toy back, screaming, or starting a fist fight. It signals that something is uncomfortable and needs to be addressed.

There's a version of the Serenity Prayer that I think is particularly helpful here:

God, grant me the serenity
To accept the people I cannot change,
The courage to change the one I can,
And the wisdom to know that's me.

This applies to your child and to you. Instead of blaming your children, your partner, or your work situation, turn the attention to yourself: *Yes, I'm feeling stressed out. What can I do now to reduce my stress and produce a better outcome?*

When you teach your children to take responsibility for themselves, you are giving them the tools to become empowered. This means that as they grow they will come to accept that life throws stressful situations in their path, and, more importantly, they will know how to deal with them.

QUESTION & ANSWER

Michelle: One of the things we didn't cover in this chapter is managing finances, and how finances can work for you as a parent, rather than against you. I know this can be an especially stressful topic for parents, because it is a part of everyday life. Can you give us some insight on how we can use the three-legged stool of being calm, confident, and focused to be successful with money as it relates to parenting?

Dr. B: I would say that that the Focus "leg" is the most important one to start with. What are your goals, and what are your resources? Living outside one's means is very stress-producing for the simple reason that it creates a disconnection. Always remember that disconnection causes stress. Racking up credit card bills is a formula for disconnection. There's no money actually there, the objects you buy are accumulating, and so are the impossibly high interest rates. Credit cards give the illusion of money, but really, the only thing that is actually there is a big fat interest rate, which will cause you intense worry and stress.

When you are about to purchase something, no matter how small or large, take a moment to consider your goal: *live within your means.* Then you can use the tools. If you consider purchasing a particular object, first: *Stop!* Ask yourself the question, *Is this taking me to my goal of living within my means?* Next: *Listen.* You'll get an inner direction that will put you back on track ("Save for it and purchase it at a later time."), and then: *Fulfill* the direction of the voice—follow through. Save your money and wait.

How does all of this relate to parenting? When you treat finances in a present, *real*, way you are showing your children long-term values and positive, lasting, healthy effects, rather than instant gratification that has no lasting satisfaction. Isn't it better to have a life that is calm, confident, and focused, than one based on getting what you want right now, only to have to pay severely for it later?

And a final note, as I was contemplating the answer to Michelle's question, I was out driving and saw this bumper sticker. Though it's not about money per se, it certainly does resonate:

> *The most important thing you can spend with your children is your time.*

CHAPTER 9

Stressed Out!

THE PATH TO SUCCESS

After working with parents and their families for over forty years, I have seen some extremely—if not excruciatingly—challenging family situations, from families on welfare struggling to put a decent meal on the table, to families that have full-time cooks. And if you think that the families with no money are the challenged ones, think again. Money does not guarantee happiness. I've worked with parents from very well-off families where there is a deep unhappiness and painful lack of support, and families with the most meager means where love and encouragement blossom every day.

Whatever your family circumstances are, I want you to remember something I said at the beginning of the book. The conditions of your life may change, but you are always you. You are the one who has to function, and function well, whatever your family circumstances are like. The good news is that as a parent you have a great influence on your family. Your family structure and its emotional landscape are yours, and while you often can't change them, you can influence them as you work on yourself, using the tools of the three-legged stool.

We have discussed in detail throughout this book how you can use the three-legged stool model to become calm in your body, confident in your mind, and focused in your spirit. These three legs are a very dynamic trio. Each leg depends on the other. If one is weak, they all suffer. If one leg is strong, they are all strengthened.

We have covered the tools of parenting success in the order of calm, confident, and then focused. However, it's not a rigid structure. You can use the tools in any order. If you need extra confidence in yourself so that you can tell your teenager she can't go out with friends, then use the confidence tools. You don't have to breathe first. If you find yourself hiding from your children in a corner—too much whining from the teenager, no time for yourself, not enough money to pay the doctor bills—maybe it's time to make use of the focus tools. If you're too angry to talk to your child about their blatant disobedience, breathe. Follow your spirit, make some new goals, and stick with them. This is a dynamic system: the three legs of the stool—body, mind, spirit—are integrally connected. No matter which leg you start with, it will lead you to the other two.

As you begin your parenting transformation keep an open communication with your child and your partner. Do your best to be a model of success for them. Show them what it means to be successful when life is challenging. As they begin to see your consistent efforts as a parent and partner, hopefully they will see and feel the love that drives you to succeed, and they will emulate that.

Life is a process. When you think you have things figured out, that is about the time something changes. There is always adjusting in the unstable world of parenting. No matter how organized you are, no matter how well you follow through, no matter how much you love your children, stress will be ever present in your life.

My co-author Michelle says:

Even with my use of the tools, stressful parenting situations continue to bombard me. My kids still have tantrums, sometimes I forget things that are important to my children, injuries are prevalent, and work still takes time away from kids. Simply put, life continues, and when I remember to use the tools and continually deepen my practice of them, I am able to reduce the stress I feel, and channel that energy to work for me as a parent, rather than against me.

Just the other day I was making a batch of homemade salsa for a party. My youngest son Jackson wanted to help. He is a fantastic button pusher, which works out since I make my salsa in the blender. He did a great job pulsing all of the ingredients. When we were done. I took the lid off and we had a taste test. It was even yummier than usual. I turned around to grab a container to pour the salsa in. As I spun back around I was splattered with tomato, cilantro, peppers, and onions. I'll let you imagine the scene. I literally took a quick chest breath—the fight or flight one. I was startled, and just about to yell, "What are you doing, Jackson?! Why did you push the button with the lid off?" when I remembered—breath, just breath. Then I told myself, "It's okay. You've seen worse. It's nothing we can't clean up."

I had an immediate turn around in my emotions, and I was in control. I ran to my room to grab the camera. This had to be captured! Everyone in the house was laughing, everyone but poor, sopping Jackson. He was covered in salsa and tears, and was stripping off his clothing. I was thankful that I remembered to use the calming breath and confidence tools, as it allowed me to focus on the humor of the situation and sooth my young son.

I love Dr. B's program. I could tell you story after story of the stressful parenting situations that happened just this week. Every time I used the tools I felt happy, successful, and fulfilled as a parent. When I didn't use the tools—like when my daughter's kindergarten class went to the zoo and I didn't go with them (because I was sure I needed to work), I was sad, restless, and full of regret. I had not listened to my spirit, and I knew it. I became even more certain that the next time I would listen to my spirit and use the tools. The program is solid. No matter what parenting throws at you, even when you make mistakes, success will come as you continue to work at it.

Michelle is right. The key to success for any parent is remembering to use the tools, and using them again and again, even when you make mistakes. And you will make mistakes. Being a parent is the hardest thing you will ever do, and I'm here to tell you that it's okay not to be perfect. It is progress we are striving for, not perfection. The key is to learn from your mistakes, and when you make new mistakes, learn from those too. Always remember, that you can refer back to the book as many times as you need. True, lasting success as a parent will require change on your part, and real change takes time. It also takes the "3 P's": patience, persistence, and perseverance.

You can do it!

Enjoy the process, and be grateful for the transformation.

About the Authors

BEN BERNSTEIN

Ben Bernstein, PhD, is a psychologist, teacher, and performance coach whose career has spanned forty years in education, psychology, and the arts, including coaching in such diverse settings as psychiatric hospitals, prisons, primary schools, and universities. He was invited to be a resource artist at the Sundance Institute, where he worked one-on-one with writers who subsequently went on to win Pulitzer Prizes, Tony Awards, and Academy Awards. He lives in the San Francisco Bay Area.

MICHELLE PACKARD

Michelle Packard, author of *Family Ever After*, graduated from Brigham Young University with a degree in Home and Family Science. She is married to the man of her dreams and sweet heart of twelve years. She readily admits that date night is her absolute favorite! Michelle is the mother of four adventurous kids with one more on the way.

She loves all things family, and especially relishes the time she has to play, work, craft, or just simply be with her kids. Floral design, historical fiction, daily walks—preferably in the mountains—music, and socializing are her personal indulgences. She enjoys cooking healthy natural foods, though she admits to a more than occasional clemency of the sweets.

She loves people and loves to see them find happiness. To learn more about Michelle check out her blog *All Things Family* at www.defendfamily. blogspot.com.

About Familius

Welcome to a place where mothers are celebrated, not compared. Where heart is at the center of our families, and family at the center of our homes. Where boo boos are still kissed, cake beaters are still licked, and mistakes are still okay. Welcome to a place where books—and family—are beautiful. Familius: a book publisher dedicated to helping families be happy.

VISIT OUR WEBSITE: WWW.FAMILIUS.COM

Our website is a different kind of place. Get inspired, read articles, discover books, watch videos, connect with our family experts, download books and apps and audiobooks, and along the way, discover how values and happy family life go together.

JOIN OUR FAMILY

There are lots of ways to connect with us! Subscribe to our newsletters at www.familius.com to receive uplifting daily inspiration, essays from our Pater Familius, a free ebook every month, and the first word on special discounts and Familius news.

BECOME AN EXPERT

Familius authors and other established writers interested in helping families be happy are invited to join our family and contribute online content. If you have something important to say on the family, join our expert community by applying at:

www.familius.com/apply-to-become-a-familius-expert

GET BULK DISCOUNTS

If you feel a few friends and family might benefit from what you've read, let us know and we'll be happy to provide you with quantity discounts. Simply email us at specialorders@familius.com.

Website: www.familius.com

Facebook: www.facebook.com/paterfamilius

Twitter: @familiustalk, @paterfamilius1

Pinterest: www.pinterest.com/familius

The most important work

you ever do will be within the

walls of your own home.

CPSIA information can be obtained
at www.ICGtesting.com
Printed in the USA
FSHW01n0436080918
52063FS